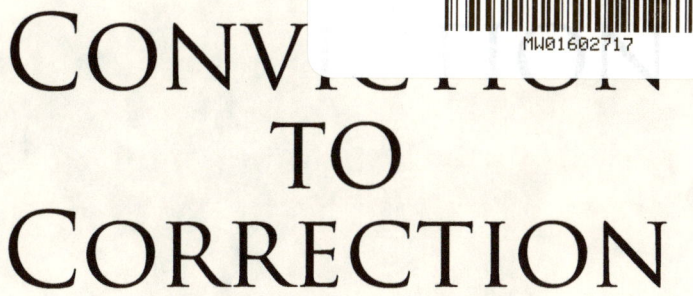
CONVICTION
TO
CORRECTION

Beyond the Walls

"Never Say Never or Surely Not Unless You Are Confident in Your Own Ability or Character"

Takasha Stevenson

ISBN 978-1-63844-483-1 (paperback)
ISBN 978-1-63844-484-8 (digital)

Christian Faith Publishing
832 Park Avenue
Meadville, PA 16335
www.christianfaithpublishing.com

Printed in the United States of America

To my beautiful grandmother, Dorothy "Doll" Billingsley. To see how you have aged gracefully at the age of eighty and yet you still manage to get around on your own with little help is a blessing from God. Thank you for continuously showing examples of moral, spiritual, and emotional support to me. I love you.

To my father, Lee Curtis Billingsley. Looking back over the past forty years of my life, I've felt a tremendous amount of pain and hurt from you. But through it all, know that you are still honored, forgiven, and loved by me.

To my beautiful mother, Henrietta "Retta" Stevenson Whatley. Do you not recognize my face anymore? It is because deep down on the inside I've changed and grown up now. Looking back over the past forty-years of my life, there was a slow transformation in our relationship because of my upbringing. My vision was fogged, and all I could see in your character was power, strictness, hostility and regret. As of today, I realized how I had misjudged you because your power has taught me how to successfully lead. Your strictness has taught me discipline. Your hostility has taught me to smile through it all. Lastly, your regret told me it's not me that you didn't want but you had regrets about choosing the wrong man as my father who left you all alone at the age of fifteen to raise me alone. Throughout all of this, I have learned responsibility and how to hold myself and others accountable. Love you!

To my stepfather, Orlando "Terrell" Whatley. I can truly say that you were a gift sent from God to mend the broken relationship between my mom and I without even knowing. You are a perfect role model to mimic when it comes to aiding and assisting your family on how to become financially stable and to leave a legacy for the next generation to come. Love you!

To my son, Richard "RJ" Moore Jr., and daughter, Wesleyana "Wes" Tubbs. It is with my deepest sympathy that I regret leaving you both. I can't imagine the pain you two felt of having both parents incarcerated at the same time. But now that I am free. The chains are broken, and the generational curses of imprisonment will end with me. But in order for us to now win at winning, every challenge that comes your way needs self-effort, and I'll be behind you both, pushing you over every obstacle, distraction or intrusion that gets in the way. Love you, kiddos!

To my one and only granddaughter, Akiylah Camille "Kiy Kiy" Moore, you are so precious, and I hold you so close to my heart. With God's help, I'm going to guard, protect, support and love you every day of your life.

It is because of you all that I now hold myself accountable, and I accept responsibility for my past. I will exceed, I must exceed, and I am going to succeed for each of you. Yes, I was wrongfully convicted, but I am back now with a vengeance in my heart against all those who oppressed me to show you how God has turned my bad into good. I will be great, I will be excellent, and I will excel in life with the favor of my Lord upon me.

To everyone who has been through any kind of setback in life, know that no matter how life beats you down, that you can always get back up, and the comeback will be major.

Contents

Prayer

Dear Lord in heaven, some days I have no idea how it'll get done, but I just know that every single day, it gets done with your help. I have truly learned from you that everything happens for a reason, and that reason causes changes that we are sometimes unable to change and are uncomfortable with. It was so hard when everything around me seemed to be falling apart, and then you showed me that everything was actually falling into place.

On days I wanted to give up, you would lift my burdens so that I could work on my moods and improve my thoughts to get myself together for the next bigger opposition that would come up against me. Whether I am sick or healthy, distressed or peaceful, in bondage or free, I know you will bring me through because my redeemer lives. In Jesus's name, I pray. Amen.

Prayer

Dear Lord God in heaven, if you never give me anything else, I will not complain because you have already given me more than I deserve. Thank you for those you placed around me to transform my thinking and then my behavior. "Iron does sharpen iron." Thank you for allowing me to suffer because my suffering was good for me, and it taught me how to obey your laws first over the laws of the land. I now trust you in every area of my life even when I don't understand because I have learned that situations are only temporary.

Regardless of how I may feel, I will rejoice each day I'm alive because it's a blessing to be amongst the living. Please give me strength and courage as I surrender all my burdens to you, Lord, going forth. All I ask you for is your shoulder to lean on, and when it's too heavy, just pick me up and carry me on. Amen

Preface

I was never prepared for half of what I went through, but somehow with God's help, I had finally made it through the storm. While I was in prison, I had begged and begged God for my freedom, and I had made lots of promises about what I would do after my release. Surely, I would do this or that for you, God, when I touch down or I would never do this or that again. I had vowed to God that I would let him fight all my battles, and I had vowed to get vengeance against my enemies and this unfair, biased, and prejudiced justice system by becoming successful.

I had thought that he had removed all my anger and my heart was pure because I had opened up to him about all my secrets and coverings. I thought that I could put the former things behind me and welcome the new things that would come for I was made new again after rededicating my life to the Lord while I was in prison. I had vowed to praise God during the bad, hard, and tough times and that I would go to church every Sunday, bible studies once a week, and to all revival services in between. I was not going to be impressed by money again or by a job title but by the way people would treat me from now on. I had vowed to never live above my means ever again because I have now survived with little.

After my release from Greenville Prison Camp and I had touched down on Alabama soil, little did I know that the enemy was waiting on me. I thought that I had forgiven all of my codefendants until I laid eyes on each of them except for two as this book was being written. *Tim,* whom I still had not seen, and I've been out almost four years now because he lives in Tuscaloosa and I live in Birmingham, and *Sherman* is still locked up and hasn't been released from prison yet. All the painful memories of how they sent me to prison and away from my children had come back to haunt me when I did see them. I had entertained certain old friendships from my past, and I saw that some of them had not changed, and they had also not accepted but questioned my change.

I had family and friends who tried to help me but came to find out they had hurt me and made things worse because it was conditional, and they also had something to gain from helping me. Real help comes from the heart and not with stipulations nor do they change with a conditional agreement in the middle of an agreement after the agreement has been made. But if you do want to change an agreement, at least give prior notice and not require the change to take effect right away.

After issues like this had started happening to me, I started to get more focused, and my prayers to God became more sincere because I had let my guard down with people once again. Trust is a dangerous thing to play with. So when you have earned or received my trust, you should feel special because after all I have been through, it's really hard for me to give out more than one free handout now.

I was told that confusion comes from how someone sees you and/or how they want you to be. I truly see people as they are and not how I want them to be because that also could be disappointing in the end as well if they don't live up to my expectations of them. Who I was and what I did were two separate things because I was not my mistake. I simply just made the wrong choices in life and went down the wrong path by hanging out with people who were not for me but had something to gain from my being in bad situations. But now that I was free again, I was not going to let my past hold me back from all the opportunities that were awaiting me in my future. I walk with confidence and not arrogance because God had given me a glimpse of my future when I was in prison, and oh my God, I can tell you that I was and still am amazed at times because my dreams are playing out little by little each day by coming to reality.

I never could have imagined myself getting a paralegal diploma from Stratford Institute and being able to attend college courses at Greenville Christian College while incarcerated. Since my release from prison, I have been working on the same job at Lear Corporations in Tuscaloosa, Alabama. I also work part-time at Serious Injury Law Group as a paralegal clerk. I obtained an associate's degree in business administration from Lawson State Community College, in Birmingham, Alabama, on May 7, 2020. I also earned another associate's degree in business office management tech/Paralegal at Shelton State Community College in Tuscaloosa, Alabama, on May 8, 2021, because of my employer's Lear Corporation tuition reimbursement opportunity program. I'm currently working toward a bachelor's degree in criminal justice at Miles College in Birmingham, Alabama, so that I can enter law school in the spring of 2023.

I'm currently working toward a bachelor's degree to enter law school in 2022, and I'm writing books that will generate into movies about my life stories and experiences to help my community and others around me. I am a living witness, and I'm here to tell you today that what the enemy had meant for harm, God had now turned into good for me. My attitude during my imprisonment has now proved my understanding of God and who He was, so I now know that he may have not come when I wanted him to, but He was always on time. I now go through trials and hardships in life with a different attitude because I know that God gives the toughest battles to his strongest soldiers.

> "For I know the plans I have for you" declares
> the Lord, "Plans to prosper you and not to harm
> you, plans to give you hope and a future."

—Jeremiah 29:11

Acknowledgments

To my Lord and Savior Jesus Christ, thank you for all you have done, are doing, and will do in others' life through me! I want to thank two of my best friends, Tara Lee Rutledge and Cynthia Williams. The type of help you ladies have given me was one a mother would give their child. I am still beyond blessed, and when I think back over the time that I've been home, I just have to wave my hand or stomp my feet sometimes when I'm alone because you two have bent over backward for me with your cash flow, transportation, housing, and credit. Wow, what a God we serve!

I want to thank my cousin/sister Tenika Stevenson for helping me with my daughter while my busy lifestyle went from normal to overworked and lacking in rest real quick. You stepped in voluntarily and assisted me with my daughter so that I could work all the long overtime hours I needed to become financially stable, and I was able to go to school to accomplish my education goals and receive two degrees in business.

I want to thank one of my close friends, Shervon Moore, for each time she invited me out to dinner or a bar. She would pay because she knew I wasn't financially stable enough to go out and enjoy myself just yet after my release but she wanted my company.

I want to thank one of my besties, Tracey Rultlege Sanders, for never saying no each time I needed to borrow money; and when she didn't have it, she made sure her husband, Charles "Punch" Sanders, loaned it to me.

I want to thank one of my favorite cousins/brothers from another mother, Michael Hopkins, because whenever I needed him, he was always there and he would sometimes come to me if I couldn't get to him. And even though we lived an hour or so away, he never said no.

I want to thank one of my best male friends in the whole wide world, Tonio Foster, because he doesn't care what I needed, he would make it happen and would always volunteer to foot the bill when there was an event because he knew I wanted to go but wasn't financially stable yet!

I want to thank a good friend of mine, Ernie Norfleet, because even after my release when he saw me, he would always ask if my daughter and I were straight or in need of anything.

I want to thank Stephanie Phillips for going out of her way to take my daughter to school because of my work schedule, which was supposed to be for two weeks and ended up being five weeks. You don't know how I'll forever be grateful to you because even though we didn't see or talk to each other on the regular, you made it happen, girl. Even when I can't be there for you, honey, I will make a way and put you first because what you did for me and my daughter was an act of kindness and a good deed.

I want to thank Jeff Tubbs for loaning me tuition money to go to school my first semester after my financial aid was gone. You didn't have to do it, but you did, and your sweet wife Joahcandra (a.k.a. Gwana) didn't mind also. It is because of you that I didn't have to prolong my education goals for lack of funding.

I want to thank two of my best friends, Janika "Nikki" West and Lacretia Lee Heard. You two know just how to give a girl a powerful and motivational speech when I was down. And I didn't even have to mention to you I was down. Your encouraging words would lift me up!

I want to thank Lachica England Taylor and Kimberly Griffin for each and every time you have come in my inbox and lifted my spirit to know you took time out of your busy days to say hello and make sure all was well with me on several occasions.

And I can't forget you either, Giovanna "Lady Childs" Howard or Hal Kynard; I feel you. You all celebrated my accomplishments along with me as if they were yours!

I want to thank a close friend of mine, "Big Ed." We became great friends after my release because of what I had gone through and I was a young single mother. He stepped in and looked out for me and my daughter, and he also gave me the down payment for my first car!

Thank you, Lashanda Woods Murphy, for keeping me in practice for law school with all this back-and-forth debating!

I want to thank my daughter's half sister, Kaneishia Smith, for her generosity and always checking on me while she was battling congestive heart failure. May you rest in peace, sweet angel.

I want to thank my daughter's half brother, Devron Smith, because he volunteered to purchase my daughter's bed when we moved into our first apartment after my release. It was common sense that I needed help with furniture. Boy, this will never go unnoticed, and if I got it, you got it!

I want to thank my son Richard "Rj" Moore for stepping up and helping me with my daughter, who is his baby sister. It was not your job; but because you were financially able and her father was absent, you assisted with her needs such as school, birthdays, holidays, and even her unnecessary petty wants.

I want to thank my TeTe, Sarah Anne, for opening up her home to me and allowing me to stay there on my weekend passes from the halfway house and my last thirty days of home confinement.

I want to thank my TeTe Thelma Billingsley Jones for cosigning for me a car while I was unable to purchase it myself due to financial hardships after my incarceration. I love you!

I want to thank my TeTe Sherri "Billingsley" Moore for your weekly check-ups, girl, and your thought-provoking speeches; my TeTe Barbara "Jean" Howze for being my loudest cheerleader and my number-one fan; and my cousin Shekera Cymon Moore for helping me with my business endeavors!

Thank you Joey Williams, my boss, for all the times you covered for me when I left work at ADESA Car Auction early to find an apartment!

Reneta Foster Johnson, who's truly an inspiration to me. Girl, I'm so proud of you! Thank you for introducing your husband

TAKASHA STEVENSON

Dorrian Johnson to me. I tell you when God has a plan, He will place the right people around you or in your life for His purpose to be fulfilled, which was Gerald Brooks, who also gave me a wonderful opportunity although I had no paralegal or office experience at all. It is because of you guys I'll remain loyal and be forever grateful.

If anyone has any injuries such as car accidents, workers' compensation, or hospital claims, don't hesitate to call the Serious Injury Law Group at 205-206-7070 and we'll be happy to take care of any claims and/or lawsuits for you!

I want to thank Donial Coleman for your guidance and always keeping me on the right track whenever I start to doubt myself and want to go left. You continue to remind me to treat life as having one-way streets and to choose them wisely because once I take a road, I cannot go in reverse.

I am personally convinced because of you, my secret admirer, that I can live with no limitations. I'm doing things now I never believed I would. You've become my safe place and told me to be authentic and live with no fear of judgement. So it's because of you that I took the mask off and I crowned myself queen! I love you, baby.

Free my big homie, Johnny "Tag" Edwards. If the justice system was really designed for rehabilitation, it shouldn't take a lifetime. I'm a living example!

Last but not the least of all, to my mother, Henrietta Stevenson Whatley, and stepfather, Orlando Terrell Whatley. The assistance you gave to my daughter will always be appreciated because the help you gave to her was a financial burden lifted off of me.

It is because of each of you that I've acknowledged to the public in this book that the overwhelming burdens were lifted off of me and you were able to help me carry loads that had become too heavy. I want to thank all of you who had my back because each of you played a major part in my transformation. Thanks for having my back when I couldn't. May God bless you all and you all continue to be a blessing to others!

To those I left behind, if any of you feel I have left you out but felt you too should have been recognized and acknowledged and for

18

whatever reason I chose not to, it is because you all were lessons and not blessings, so I didn't feel the need to expose you! Instead of revealing you, I walked away from the lies, manipulation, and deceit that left me crying and feeling empty from you all. I wanted to bring you all along with me; but you allowed yourselves to be used as obstacles in my life to hurt, ridicule, lie, and mock me! I took away growth and maturity from those lessons. So to those I've left behind, my enemies, naysayers, haters, and even my frenemies, it was all because of the roles you played that I am a changed person. I have now learned to forgive without revenge!

Introduction
Why Should You Read This Book?

The reason that you should read this book is because it has some amazingly shocking truths that could be similar to yours, and it could give you insight and hope to press on. It can help inspire you to become who God created you to be. When we experience trials in our lives, don't be so quick to give up, but instead, pray, believe, and keep the faith, and God will reveal his purpose for you in life. Circumstances are temporary, and therefore, they can change at any time. God can remove, change or help you overcome any situation because you are not your mistake, past or environment. Go to God with all your burdens and not people because it is a process, and people will let you down along the way. Take it from the chapters in this book!

Preventative Measure

People are who they are, so when they show you who they are, please believe them. When they show you inconsistency, inconsideration, disloyalty, ungratefulness, entitlement or just behave in ways that disturbs your peace, then those are the wrong people to have around you.

Real people are rare and are hard to find, so if you know of any, you better level up to keep them in your life. Choose people who choose you. There's something about a realist, and they have a glow to them because they are not hating, bitter, messy or plotting evil against you or anyone else.

Today I can honestly say to anyone that I am blessed with everything I need. I am working hard toward everything I want to achieve in life, and I am most appreciative and grateful for all that I have in life.

Message to My Hometown

The system was designed to keep those who are down at the bottom and for those who are at the top to keep rising. No one can take care of a community better than those who reside there or those who have come from there. Let's come up with a plan to work together to keep Marion, Alabama, moving forward. We have great people who have come from there or who have come through there.

The late Jimmy Lee Jackson was a black civil rights activist who marched alongside the late Dr. Martin Luther King Jr. for blacks to have equal rights and the right to vote. He was born on December 16, 1938, and was raised in Marion, Alabama. On February 18, 1965, he was protesting along with his sister, mother, and eighty-two-year-old grandfather when he was shot at Mack's Cafe in Marion, Alabama, by a white state trooper for protecting his mother from being beaten. And he later died on February 26, 1965 in Selma Alabama. For those who live there now and don't know, Rollins Funeral Home sits where Mack's Cafe once resided.

Albert Turner Elementary School was named after the late Albert Turner Sr., a civil rights activist and advisor to the late Dr. Martin Luther King Jr. He was born on February 29, 1936, and he died on April 13, 2000, from health complications. The late Coretta Scott King was born on April 27, 1927, in Heiberger, Alabama, just up the road, about ten minutes outside Marion. She was an activist who advocated for African-American equality, an author, and a civil rights leader alongside her husband, the late Dr. Martin Luther King Jr., whom she married on June 18, 1953. And he was murdered on April 4, 1968. She died on January 30, 2006, from a stroke in which she had suffered from August of 2005, and it had left her unable to speak. And five months later she had complications from ovarian cancer and respiratory failure.

I stated all of that to say this: "Great leadership isn't about controlling someone." It's about empowering those who feel powerless, inspiring those who are uninspired, encouraging those who are discouraged, and helping those who are in need and can't help themselves. Our town is very small, and most of the people who live here are relatives of some kind. So why can't we all get along with one another, help one another, and live peaceful lives?

We must learn to live together or perish together as fools.

—Dr. Martin Luther King Jr.

Exodus

As I walked out the door toward the gate that would
lead to my freedom, I knew If I didn't leave my
bitterness and hatred behind, I'd still be in prison.

—Nelson Mandela

Leaving Greenville prison camp had me so excited on the inside I could hardly contain myself. I had so much rushing through my mind like where would I work, live, drive, and would I even be able to survive as a felon. I was financially unprepared for the free world because I had nothing but my thirty-five-dollar debit card in which the prison had given me to eat with on my bus ride home to Alabama. But I knew somehow that God was going step in if I step aside and let him.

I was taking with me some of the inspiring messages from a few of the ladies at the prison camp and had now planned to live a prosperous and fulfilling life. I have learned from my mistakes, and now I plan to serve my purpose! The measure of my success now is the quality of life I live, which is my personality, character, integrity, attitude, and loyalty. I had now been released from Greenville Federal Prison camp to the custody of the Federal Halfway House in Birmingham, Alabama, on October 2, 2017. I had learned an important lesson while I was away, which consisted of: stop trying to beat the law but instead abide by it.

I was returning into a society now that had not stopped or slowed down but instead, felt like it had sped up, and it was hard trying to get back on track and especially keep up in it. I had so many plans and goals that I had promised myself and God I would keep, but to be honest, when I sniffed that little bit of freedom air, I knew it was impossible. Almost every promise that I had made to God and myself while I was in prison I have failed since being out. I was like God. I knew what I had said I was going to do, but please forgive me for what I'm about to do.

After realizing this now, I never say never unless I am confident in my own ability and strength because I've broken almost every promise I made to God before my release. I remember getting into the prison van to be transported to the bus station, and my eyes were watery after hugging and waving goodbye to my fellow inmates and newfound friends that I was leaving behind. I told the prison bus driver that my heart was pounding and I couldn't believe that this day had finally arrived after seeing so many others go before me.

I laid my head back onto the headrest and prayed to God all the way to the bus station, holding back tears of joy because I didn't want to cry in front of her. And plus, I wanted to focus on the motion sickness I was feeling for not being able to ride in a vehicle but a few times out of thirty months, and when I did it was for transit to Greenville College for classes. After arriving at the bus station, I hugged the driver goodbye, and then she drove off. After being incarcerated thirty months, it felt so weird integrating back into a society of free people.

As I walked through the bus station, I stared and gazed at people to see who looked friendly enough to let me use their cell phone so that I could call and see where my ride to Clarksville, Tennessee, was parked. I spotted this elderly man who looked as if he was in his late fifties, and I asked if he'd mind me using his phone to call my ride. And of course, he said yes. I had on street clothing, so he didn't know that I had just been released from prison.

When I spotted JJ's car, I ran over and gave him a big hug and said, "Let's get on the highway now before someone sees me."

He said, "After all this time you served, I thought you would have wanted something to eat first since you went without the food of your choice."

I said, "I do but away from this town so that I could feel safer."

I did not ride the bus to the halfway house, and I threw my bus ticket away in the garbage at the bus station. I had JJ to pick me up so that I could spend long hours riding home with my family instead of being stuck on a stuffy and stinky bus ride. The reason people lie and say we are riding the bus is because we would rather spend those long hours in a car with family and friends instead of on a crowded bus with strangers.

It's not that we want to get in some type of trouble, but that you will get longer hours riding a bus instead of in a car to spend our first twenty-four hours with family because sometimes a bus has stops and layovers and all those hours count as extra time to arrive at the halfway house, depending on how far you have to go. And with the layovers, some people get up to forty-eight hours to get there by bus. I used JJ's phone, and I called my kids to see how far away they were because I was going to meet them, my cousin, and best friend in Clarkesville, Tennessee, which was halfway between Greenville, Illinois, and Birmingham, Alabama.

We arrived in St. Louis, Missouri, on South Jefferson Avenue at a Lee's Chicken about an hour later outside of Greenville, Illinois, and I couldn't wait to eat. I thought I would be excited about the chicken, but instead, I was still more anxious and awaiting to reunite with my kids. I used JJ's phone halfway down the highway talking to old friends until I realized I was barely talking to him. So I got off and talked with him a little while before I got out of his car because this was so generous of him to do this for me. I remember after arriving at some gas station in Clarkesville, Tennessee, my ride to Alabama was late as usual.

I called and said, "Get here now and stop lying to me about your whereabouts. This is serious, and I could get into trouble if I'm seen anywhere but on the bus. And yes, people have been caught at stores or restaurants in which they were supposed to be on the bus and had to go back to the prison and serve their sentencing to the end."

They had finally pulled up, and I jumped out the car, and I ran and jumped into each of their arms one by one. I think JJ was more happy to see me reunite with my kids just as much as I was. I said my goodbyes to JJ, hugged him, and thanked him for taking time out of his busy schedule to come visit every other weekend and for bringing me halfway to Alabama.

He said, "I wouldn't have missed this moment for nothing in the world, Kasha, being that I lived right next door in St. Louis beside Greenville, Illinois. You and my sister have been friends since kids, and I know she's proud of me for doing this as well."

We stayed at the gas station about another thirty minutes playing lottery tickets before leaving. We talked, laughed, and reminisced all the way down the busy highway, and everyone was loud trying to out-talk each other. Pokey handed me a prepaid cell phone with a camera on it to talk and text on my ride home, and of course, you know I took pictures and sent them so friends could see that I was out.

We arrived in Birmingham, Alabama around 2:00 a.m. and stopped by Walmart and picked up sleeping clothes and a couple pairs of comfortable outfits for the halfway house. I was dropped off at my Aunt Sarah's house around 4:00 a.m., and my friends, Diddy and Giovanna, came over to see me for about thirty-minutes. After they left, I had gone into the house and lounged onto my aunt's sofa and finally dozing off. I received a phone call from my best friend, Janika.

"Get up, heffa. It's time to go to the halfway house."

I replied, "I have two more hours."

And she said, "I know, but we are going to get something to eat first. Pancakes and sausage, your favorite."

We went to Denny's and ate breakfast, took pictures, and then headed to the halfway house. I was late because a train had stopped on the tracks in our route there. I called to the halfway house to let them know.

And they said, "We are already aware because some others have called ahead of you, but thanks for checking in to us because we will put an escape charge on you for being late as fast as a two-year-old getting on YouTube. We don't tolerate that."

After hanging up the phone, I thought to myself about asking Janika to go elsewhere, but nah, I'm going to do right. The train finally moved, and we headed straight to the halfway house. Pulling into the parking lot on October 3, 2017 around 8:30 a.m., I thanked Janika for transporting me there. We both grabbed two bags a piece, and it was then as I started walking I realized I had transitioned into a world of freedom and was now exiting and leaving my past life of incarceration behind me.

I said to Janika (in my "Tiffany Haddish" voice) right before we entered into the halfway house, "Free at last. Free at last. Now that I'm out, I'm gone shake this big azz."

The hardest prison to escape is your mind.

—Unknown

Dependent

Whenever you do something for someone, especially volunteer help, do it from the heart because if not, sometimes you can hurt them or the relationship more than you can help them.

—Takasha L. Stevenson

From the moment that I had walked into the halfway house, I had to be dependent on someone at all times because at this point, there was nothing that I could get done for myself as of yet. Have you ever needed help because you couldn't do something for yourself and someone else had to do it or it wouldn't get done?

After being checked into yet another FBOP system, I was assigned to a dorm with two other ladies. I had a twin bed, same as in prison, but this time, it had a real twin mattress on it instead of a plastic mat that kids have in kindergarten or head start for their naptime. And I had a locker four times the size of the one I had in prison. The bathroom had two toilets, three showers, but only two worked, five sinks with mirrors, two washers, and two dryers. The facility had their own cleaning supplies, but everything else, I had to purchase on my own.

I had come out of prison with only thirty-five dollars on a debit card because that is what the prison had given me to eat with for two meals on my supposedly bus ride to Birmingham, Alabama, which was supposed to be a ten-to-twelve-hour bus ride with one layover. Before leaving, Janika had to take my talk-and-text cell phone that Pokey had brought me back with her because it had a camera on it. So she went and purchased me a talk-and-text-only prepaid phone without a camera. When she arrived back, I thanked her over and over again and told her how appreciative I was and that I would pay her back someday. She had already paid for my breakfast and now a cell phone because she understood that it was crucial for me to have contact with my kids and/or to handle my business now that I was out of prison.

The administrator did not check in the cell phone right away for whatever reason, so I called my kids on the facility phone and told them I had made it and I would call them a little later when my phone was checked in because you could only use the facility phone no more than fifteen minutes at a time. My son had to go to work my first weekend there, so he wasn't able to come and visit because he had just started a new job. I talked with my mom, and she had to work the upcoming weekend also, so she couldn't come. But Pokey and her kids, my daughter, and my grandbaby had come to visit me my first weekend there.

Pokey dropped the kids off and went and got us some food to eat because on the weekend, we could have whatever food we wanted. I was so happy because I didn't have any money for real to buy anything. But they were spoiling me anyways for my return home. Pokey had brought a few of my old clothing along with some new clothing because I had gained at least twenty-five pounds while I was away. She came back with Pizza Hut, and I ate it like a rib eye steak. Before she left, she gave me seventy-five dollars to put in my pocket to have when I went out job searching because I really didn't need any money in the halfway house. Well, at least that's what I thought in the beginning.

I was able to go to the orthodontist after being there two weeks, and an old dear friend had taken me to this appointment and also paid for it. I was also able to go and get my driver's license so that I could go out and search for a job after being there three weeks, so my friend, Diddy, came up and took me to get them, even though she was late as usual. Oh, and we went and ate afterward because I had extra time to be out.

One day I had pretended to be sick so that I could go to the doctor for a check-up because I never did trust the prison doctors. I had heard too many horror stories about the prison system, like back in the days, they would take black ladies' uterus out without permission to keep them from having kids so that they couldn't continue to populate the black race.

My good friend, Janika, had come to take me, and she would always show up early and before my check out time came, and when I would walk out the doors, she would be parked right in the doorway. I think she was one car space away from preparing to drive up in there. The third weekend, my mom and her new husband of only one month had come to visit along with my daughter, Pokey, Chelle, my Auntie Gaye, and all of their kids and grands because it was Classic weekend in Birmingham.

Classic weekend is when two black college football teams, Alabama State and Alabama A&M, would play against each other, and the town would have rappers and superstars from all over to perform during halftime and the after-parties. It was like a mini family reunion in the facility visiting area. I had now met my stepdaddy for the first time, and he seemed pretty cool. My grandbaby didn't come back this particular weekend because of all the traffic in Birmingham during this busy, eventful weekend. And my daughter didn't want to leave me, but she knew that she couldn't stay either. My mom had bought me some panties, bras, socks and some of my important papers so that I could sort through them. I was there at least three weeks by now, and I had only gone on two job searches because it was hard for me to get around with family and friends living in Marion, Alabama, which was an hour and half away. And I had no car, so I would have to wait on Janika to come on her off days.

Pokey had given me seventy-five dollars each week for four weeks to get food and necessities while I was out job searching. It was now getting to me because this wasn't her duty. Besides the panties, bras, and socks, my mom had also bought me washing powder, Clorox, fabric sheets, lotion, deodorant, and hair care two times; and she had given me forty dollars three times during my six months in the halfway house. She told me after the second time she couldn't do this anymore and that I needed a job.

I was hurt and confused at the same time because I didn't know where she had expected me to get it from. I had just gotten over being prideful during my prison bid and had now humbled myself to ask others for help because this was why I dated drug dealers or men with money so I wouldn't have to beg anyone. I didn't want to depend on a man because a man was the reason I had gotten into all this trouble (my daughter's father). So now I was going to have to depend on another man until I could do better because at least I wouldn't have to pay him back if I was dating him.

I had a guy friend to help me out here and there, but I didn't want to totally depend on him because this is when control comes in. Plus he was in the middle of a situation and wasn't all mine, if you know what I mean. I mean I had just served thirty months for money laundering, and I came home to nothing. So I could now see clearly why so many felons get out and go back into the system because they have to provide for themselves the best they can with what they have, and that is nothing. So we then have to go back to our old way of getting money and take chances on getting caught again rather than being homeless and begging.

No, it was nobody's fault but mine, but at this moment, there was nothing that I could do for myself after serving thirty months in prison. And I had at least thought that family, friends, and/or especially the ones I had helped before I went to prison would have something waiting on me because I didn't want to just beg anybody. It wasn't anybody's duty but my own to help provide for me. And plus, I was a grown woman (thirty-seven years old at this time), but in reality, I had nothing. And I couldn't even save up anything because in prison, we work and only get paid fourteen cents an hour, so you can't even save up because your hygiene care each month will take all of this and sometimes more depending on what you purchased.

One of my best friends, Cynt Williams, had come to visit me and brought me five pairs of new pants size 11/12 because I was a size 7/8 before I had gone to prison and couldn't wear my old clothing. My Aunt Sarah had told me that one of our cousins who lived in Birmingham said he would take me around when I needed him to because he knew I didn't have any other way and he didn't work because he was retired. It was so nice of him to volunteer to help me out. He came twice a week to take me job searching for about two weeks (which was a total of four times) because that's how often I could get out each week—only two times for job haunts. I offered him gas money a time or two in which Pokey had given me, but he turned it down, so I stopped offering.

After my fifth week of being there, I had finally took a job at a car auction because that's all that was hiring at the time, which was about thirty-five minutes away, and I only made eight dollars an hour. And out of that, I had to pay the facility a fee of 25 percent each week to stay in custody there or I could be sent to the county jail to stay my remainder halfway house time because policy stated you have to have a job within twenty-one days and pay 25 percent weekly because you can't live there for free unless you have a disability preventing you from working. And then you probably would have stayed your last six months in prison or got less than six months halfway house time because the halfway house is for those getting out and who are able to work and save before getting released back into society to have time to adapt so they could start with a small savings instead of coming out with a thirty-five-dollar debit card like I did after my release from prison. And you certainly can't quit or get fired from a job either or you could be sent to the county jail.

My first day of work I called my cousin about twenty times and got no answer, so I called a taxi. And he charged me forty dollars one way, and this didn't include him picking me up after I got off. So the seventy-five dollars Pokey had given me for the week was basically already gone, and might I add I was late my first day of work. I had gotten really upset, and I called once again after I had made it to work to see if he was okay or just dodging me. And my cousin answered saying that he had forgotten Monday was library day for his grandkids.

I understood that, but a library wasn't even open at six in the morning. I knew right then that our relationship was over with. And anybody else who want to defend him on this could go straight to hell behind him also because he and I had made an agreement. But if I knew that he wasn't going to follow through, I would have already made other arrangements or I wouldn't have taken the job knowing I couldn't get there.

So after this happened and in order for me to keep my job, my Aunt Sarah volunteered to pick me up and let me drop her off each day at work, and she carpooled home in the evenings with a friend for about three weeks. About a week after this, I could tell she had regretted this decision because her attitude would change some days, and she would drill me if I was late coming home. But if I started leaving the job early, I would have eventually gotten fired and sent to the county jail the remainder of my time for leaving early. And if I had gotten stopped by a police, I would have gotten sent to the county jail and could possibly face charges because I wasn't driving an authorized vehicle by the facility.

After I noticed this a couple of times, I told one of my best friends, Shay, that she had to hurry up and send all the necessary paperwork for me to be able to keep her car at the facility because she had volunteered to give me her brand new 2016 Altima to drive so that I wouldn't have any issues getting back and forth to work in a city where no one could come to my rescue on time if I broke down and was late getting back to the halfway house. This would cause me to get a written citation because they are teaching us responsibility and holding us accountable, so she drove her used car. This also was the reason my aunt had volunteered her carpooling with someone else because it was only supposed to be for a week. But due to my paperwork getting misplaced by the director in which I think was on purpose, it went on for a total of three weeks.

Shay had also discussed this with her husband, and he had no problem with this because I was her bestie. So the week of Thanksgiving, Shay had given me her car to drive back and forth to work the remainder of my time in the halfway house in which my release date wasn't until March 30, 2018. I was so grateful to have a friend like this in my life at a time like this, and little did she know but she had just received a blessing from God for her future in which He's going to bless me to bless her if it's the last thing I do.

I had other friends who had more than one car also, but do you think they volunteered it to me? Nope, they did not! I also must acknowledge this. Shay let me drive her car for free, and she had a car payment on it. I continued to have visits from other friends and family at the halfway house on weekends: Tracey Rutledge Sanders, Tonio Foster, Mike Hopkins, Cynt Williams, and Shanda Woods Murphy. I was very appreciative of them, and every time they came, they knew to bring some kind of food because I couldn't live off of visits alone.

I had a need in my life, and I had several thoughts about getting back in them streets with a dope boy, but today I can say (but God) several other friends offered money to me as well, but it was always with stipulations and conditions. So I guess it's safe to say they were never really my friends because I don't care how down or low I was. I had never been the type of chick to do something strange (sex) in exchange for some change. (Oh well. Their loss, not mine).

> God does not begin by asking us about our ability, but
> only about our availability, and if we then prove our
> dependability, He will increase our Capability!

> —Neal A. Maxwell

Distractions

When the enemy cannot destroy you, his job is to distract you.

—Unknown

My felony background was not going to be an excuse to keep me stuck in the past. I have had so much to come against me, but I would always remember the vision God had already given me. The halfway house had become extremely distracting while being there. It is supposed to help us integrate back into society, but instead, they tried to make us feel uncomfortable in our own skin. They did more hating than the prosecutor and the snitches that had put us there. From the moment I walked into the halfway house, I was already prejudged by some of the employees. Maybe because of how I was dressed after just being released from prison.

I had on an Air Jordan fitted shirt, some skintight jeans gripping my hips and nice size little azz, and I had on a pair of Nike Air Jordan shoes. Maybe they felt like I didn't look or act like a felon who had just been released and wanted me to. Still to this day, I don't know why, but I also can care less to find out why they hated me now because they can no longer hinder my success now that I am out. And besides, my worth was not measured by their liking or approval of me. I remember when I first walked into the halfway house, and I was eyeballed from head to toe by the employees and the inmates, but for two different reasons I'm sure.

We are still humans who just simply made a mistake, but we are not our mistakes. And besides, everyone who goes there has just finished serving time as a punishment, so there's no need to keep punishing us. The first time the enemy had come against me was after Janika had come back with the proper prepaid phone without a camera on it, and it was talk-and-text-only. The director, Ms. Jaye, had come out of her office and said, "Give it here. I will inspect it and release it to her after I've finished with it."

I was like, cool, and standing there waiting, and she told me to not rush her but she'll get to it. I was angry and confused because if you were not able to inspect this brand new phone in right away, which was still in the box, and it probably wouldn't have taken sixty seconds to look over, why did you come out of your office to get it? That is what I thought to myself especially when I saw other officers checking other phones in and handing it right over to the inmates. I walked away and went into my dorm room to put all my things away neatly and tried to wait patiently because by now, a few hours had passed.

I went out around 4:45 p.m. to see if the phone had been checked in because I knew Ms. Jaye would be leaving around 5:00 p.m. I respectfully knocked on her door, and she said, "Yes, ma'am. What do you want?" in a calm tone of voice.

I said, "I was wondering if you had checked the phone in so I could use it to call my children."

She responded, "Nope, and I'm not going to because you are worrying me while I'm busy. And as a matter of fact, you won't get it at all today because I'm about to leave." Then she opened her desk, put the phone in it, and locked it. I walked away teary-eyed, confused, and angry as hell because I wanted to beat her azz, and I couldn't.

I was so mad at God because he had once again allowed me to get into a situation in which I couldn't do anything about it, so I went to my room. Later on, I came out and discussed her with another employee, and their response was, "Wow. I don't know why she did that because she doesn't usually check phones in because this is apart of our job. And besides, it wouldn't have taken her twenty seconds to read the box to see what kind of phone it was and give it to you."

I had become really angry and confused at this point and was wondering where was all that coming from and was she targeting me.

I went to the office and asked to use the facility phone, and I blew smoke off to a friend to calm myself down even though I knew the phone calls were recorded on their end. I didn't care at this moment. I wanted her to hear everything I had to say about her.

The next day Ms. Jaye didn't come to work, so I went back to my dorm room, and I went into the bathroom and cried silently as I talked to myself. But of course, anyone who knows me knows that I did use the facility phone all day and night and more than the fifteen minutes they allowed us. The third day upon arrival, I spoke to Ms. Jaye as she walked out of her office, and she spoke back as if nothing had happened between us a couple days before. And of course, I did not ask her for the phone.

At the end of the day about fifteen minutes before 5:00 p.m., I was called into the office and given my phone by another employee, Ms. Bee. I thought to myself, *Why didn't Ms. Jaye give it to me herself if she's so bad.* Due to me not having a job, I wasn't allowed to go out on passes except for medical visits, job searches, and church on Sundays, which was for three hours because you cannot stop someone from serving their religious beliefs. So I sat around bored and wrote in my journals, and boy, did I have some things to write!

The second time she got at me was when I needed to go and take my driver's license. I went to her office and knocked on her door. She told me to enter. I asked about choosing a date to go and take my driver's license because my family had to drive over an hour to come and pick me up, so I needed to know ahead so they won't take off work for nothing. She told me that I wouldn't be going out the coming week because she doesn't like people coming to her, so she denied my pass. So after this time around, I had figured it all out now and not to go to her about anything just choose a date and wait on an answer.

The following week after this incident, I was approved for the date I put in for, and it was the day before my license was going to expire in which I hadn't paid attention to. So I know it was God looking out for me even when I didn't feel him. So I didn't have to take the road test again, I only went in and renewed them and left in about thirty minutes after my picture was taken and renewal fees paid. So because of her, I had about four to five more hours to hang out because you can't time how long someone would be at the DMV, so I stayed out to 5:00 p.m. because that's around the time they would be closing, and me and Diddy went and ate at Ruby Tuesday.

The third time Ms. Jaye had gotten at me was when I had gotten sick and needed to go to the doctor because of a nasty cough I had. I ended up getting a cold at the beginning of the week, and I thought maybe I had the flu because I couldn't shake the cough or the nauseous feeling in my stomach. So I went to the office and asked if I could call a friend (Janika) to take me to the emergency room. I was told nope by the director because she has to be the one to approve this while she was still at work.

She then responded, "Do you need an ambulance?"

And I said nope. I wanted my family to take me to the hospital because I didn't trust anything about the bureau system because if we die in their custody, they get compensated and not our family because each of us belongs to them and is insured by them. And on your death certificate it will state "escape by death," meaning we got away and didn't finish our sentencing because we died. So sad but true. So it's important for your family to also have insurance because they can get your body from the BOP and bury you in your family cemetery.

Mr. Danny told me that I could call someone to bring some cold and flu over-the-counter medicine, so that's what I did. My cousin who had taken me around job searching and also agreed to take me to work the first couple of weeks until my car was approved had brought the medicine to me, but of course, this was before we had fallen out about him not showing up. I laid around all day in the bed medicated. We cannot bring medicine in our rooms, so we have to go out and take it in front of an employee.

So after I had taken it the second time, which was in the afternoon, I told Ms. Bee I was about to go and shower and lay back down because she had asked me how I was feeling, and I replied, "Still bad." Ms. Jaye decided to have a fire drill around 2:00 p.m., which was a practice drill, but no one had told me after I had clearly stated I was about to shower and lay back down. The entire staff that day knew that I was sick and in bed all day because the women employees have to make rounds every hour. Soon as I got in the shower, the fire drill went off.

I was in the shower about three minutes, and I thought that it had gone off by mistake because my first week there, the fire drill had gone off three times in one week by mistake around 3:00–4:00 a.m. So I kept showering, and no one came and got me. As I rushed through my shower and came out, I could tell the building was still empty, so I hurried and dressed and went outside in the freezing cold with the others still standing in line. Everyone else was already out of the building and waiting on me angrily because they were ready to enter back into the building because they were cold but couldn't until I had come out and was counted too.

When the practice drill was over, Ms. Jaye had asked me to come into her office. I did and she wrote me a written citation for a safety hazard: ignoring a fire drill. This caused me not to go out on any passes that I had earned. I explained to her that I was in the shower and I couldn't run out with a towel wrapped around me with over fifty men living there. She stated, "If it was a real one, you would have, so start treating them all as if they are real."

She also told me that Miss. Kay had yelled out when she came in and checked the rooms, but I explained that I didn't hear her. But she wasn't listening to anything I had to say. Besides, I was sick with flu-like symptoms so why would she do this to me? She took away my passes for two weeks, and I could not go out on passes my very first weekend in which I had earned by then. I called my boo thang and told him that I couldn't go and eat dinner with him on my first approved weekend and that we had to cancel our plans on Saturday.

I had now wanted to grab this witch's broom and break it across her head. I was ready for whatever in my Master P's voice ("I'm bout it bout it"). After this had happened, I was waiting on another fire drill to happen. I probably would have stripped naked and ran out with a towel wrapped around me to see what would happen, but of course, we never had another practice fire drill again, so I felt targeted. Oh yes, and of course, the fire drill kept going off on other nights for whatever reason, but they would run to announce it was triggered by the heaters smoke and not to go outside because they're lazy selves were too cold and didn't want to count us. But the old me wanted to go out so bad and line up.

The fourth time that Ms. Jaye came at me indirectly was after about a month of having my job. My best friend, Shay, had given me all the documents I needed to get her car approved for me to drive back and forth to work. Ms. Jaye had let the paperwork sat on her desk over a week before even looking at it, and then she came to me the next week stating that she had misplaced my copies of the tag receipt, insurance card with my name on it showing that I'm a legal driver for the car, and a signed and notarized statement from Shay showing that she had given me permission to drive the car during my stay at the halfway house. And she even questioned if I had given her everything (really?).

So once again, I got all the paperwork sent back to me again through fax and gave it to her, but it took longer because Shay had to get the statement notarized again because you can't fax a notarized statement because of the seal. Oh, by this time, I felt she was playing with my livelihood, and all vengeance was mine in my mind. After this, she gave it to my caseworker, Miss Kay, to handle, and it still took two more weeks to approve this because she claimed she was behind in her paperwork already. I feel to this day she was targeting me because of the men in there. She only got attention when the men were trying to manipulate and deceive her to get more free time out on outings away from the halfway house. Plus, I had a man, and I wasn't even interested in any of the men there. But they did keep some good company and help time pass by quickly for me.

I had now been working for a couple of months, and there was a lady named Mrs. Faye who worked in accounting. She accepted all the payments and worked with us on job searches. Well, after I had come in and handed her my money order on this particular Friday, she took it and left it for me at the front office only so that I could receive it back on the next day, which was Saturday morning. I couldn't understand why she just didn't tell me it was wrong that same day. After I read it, it stated that I overpaid the facility by five cents, and all my passes for the weekend and the upcoming weekend had been suspended. I was devastated because had I known of this, I would have brought in some snacks since I couldn't leave until Sunday because I didn't eat the facility food there either, but they couldn't stop me from going out for church on Sundays.

I had lost my passes this same weekend, and I couldn't put in any for the following weekend either because I was still on punishment all because I overpaid them by five cents. She explained this would be like the government is stealing from me if they accept an overpayment, and she couldn't allow me to go back out to get it corrected because it was due Friday evening by 6:00 p.m. And that's the time I usually come in from work, so I didn't have the time to.

I was so upset with Ms. Faye, and I had blamed Ms. Jaye because I felt this was another indirect attack against me. I called my boyfriend once again to tell him what had happened but told him we were still on for Sunday. The last time was the last time that Ms. Jaye got at me indirectly because I had done had enough of her indirect small attacks and wasn't going to stand for anything else. I was ready to go to the county jail because if she had just pulled one more scheme or scandal, whatever you want to call it, I was going to give her what she kept asking for, and that's a reason for me to go back to prison because clearly, any fool could see what she was doing.

I had gone to the doctor one day because I still had not healed completely from my cough and cold with over-the-counter medicine, and I was given a prescription. I turned it in also and had to go to the front office to take it three times a day. Well, because I worked, I had to take two pills a day with me. So on this particular day, an officer decided to count my pills, and two were missing. They came and confronted me after seeing that I had two pills missing, and they had done a locker search and found one in my locker. I would take two pills a day to work with me instead of one when I left for work because I was never back in time for lunch, so I would take it while I was still at work.

They searched my locker, and I had one laying in there. I had forgotten to take it earlier, so when I got back, I laid it on the top shelf of my locker. I was going to take it later with my dinner because I had forgotten to take it on my lunch break, and besides, I had an empty stomach at the moment. They tried to write me up and wanted to send me to the county jail for abuse of medication like I was taking too many pills, giving them away or possibly selling them. I explained that I took two out a day because I wasn't there during the day to take them as needed for breakfast and lunch since I had to take them three times a day, and I didn't get back to the facility until after 7:00 p.m.

The officer who searched my room was new and had only been there about two months, so I felt this was an indirect attack, and she used a rookie to come at me because I was at work during the day. And Ms. Jaye must have missed my presence around the facility, I guess, and saw that I was walking a straight line. I felt strongly Ms. Jaye had the officer picking at me and doing a room search because she had called me into her office and questioned me about the extra pill being laid around in my locker the next day. If this was resolved the night before with a clear understanding, why was she still harassing me the very next day?

But by God's grace, he saved me once again. I feel he was trying to teach me a lesson from it all, and I failed him repeatedly because of my attitude. I hate bullying and/or picking, and surely, I don't like when it's indirect. I feel if you want me, then come at me directly so that I can have the same opportunity to jack you up like you want to do to me. I started to pray to God for the serenity prayer.

"God, please help me accept the things I cannot change but give me courage to change the things that I can," and before you knew it, my attitude toward Ms. Jaye was no longer nasty. I didn't speak to her but ignored her every move and paid her no attention, but in the back of my mind, I still wanted to snatch her up and scare the hell out of her. It may have not helped with me not speaking to her, but trust me, it didn't hurt either. Little did I know then that God was preparing me for the outside world because Lord only knows when I got released, I faced distractions worse than this that could have really sent me back to prison.

So now I don't respond to certain foolishness because I have leveled up spiritually and mentally. I had to learn that I couldn't receive the blessings God had waiting on me because I kept responding to ignorance. You would have thought I would have learned my lesson after the judge told me that "ignorance of the law was no excuse." I remember when I used to tell these stories I would still get mad, but now I don't. I may look back and wish I could change just a few things, but then I realize I would lack certain knowledge. So every now and again when I do look back, I just wave my hand, smile, and say thank you because without those horrific moments, I wouldn't have grown. Now I am open to learning new knowledge, living with no regrets, and saying thank you.

> Stop getting distracted by things that have
> nothing to do with your goals.

—Unknown

Create Who You Are

It's never too late to be what you might have been

—George Elliot

Being angry, sad, and overthinking isn't worth it anymore, and it has cost me my peace so many times in the past. After I had learned not to cry over my past because it was gone and realizing that I couldn't get it back, I stopped feeling sorry for myself because sorrow only leads to stagnation, and where there was stagnation, there was no room for growth because there was death.

While serving time in prison, I served God more than I ever have in life, and to be honest, even since I've been out. I took the Holy Bible, and I examined myself daily and found out exactly who I had become. I was a light of hope because I always believe you create your own world because I don't see the world as others do. While I was in the halfway house, one day I started studying how to control my thoughts so that I could improve my attitude because I had remembered an elderly lady from the church in prison, which I attended right before my release, had told me that our brains have memories of sound and our mouth just duplicates our thoughts. She also told me to go and live in the present, make it relevant, significant, and meaningful.

So pending my release from the halfway house to the free world, I had remembered this again, and I had promised myself to seek out and see what kind of heart God wants me to have. I had served two and a half years of my life in prison and six months in a halfway house, and now I was tired of being angry at the people who had put me there and those who had hurt me throughout life. I realized that being angry wasn't helping me, and I was only delaying or stopping the blessings God had for me. All the what-if, should-have, and could-have had now stopped, and I was stressing over my release from the halfway house.

I wanted to know where I would live and work after my release from the halfway house. I wanted to know what great jobs would possibly hire a felon. I wanted to know who would accept me and not judge me by my past. I just wanted to know if my life would ever be back to normal again. So I started praying and asking God to show himself in my life and guide me, my tongue, my footsteps, and cleanse this regretful, sinful, revengeful, and evil heart of mine because my thoughts were consuming me.

Today I've let go of meaningless relationships and those who give handouts only to expect something in return. "Perfect people are exceptional pretenders or compulsive liars one," is what I read once. I had allowed my thoughts to keep me in bondage, but as the giant inside of me had awakened, I was no longer in bondage. I wake up each morning, and at some point throughout the day when I'm reminded, I speak God's words over my life (affirmation). I speak only what I wish to have because words are like tree roots. They can nourish and strengthen you or they can come to ruin or cause stagnation (death) in your life.

> For as a man thinketh in his heart so is he.
> (Proverbs 23:7)

This scripture tells us that whatever we think, we become it.

> A man is not defiled by what enters his mouth, but by what comes out of his mouth. (Matthew 15:11)

After reading this, I started focusing my mind on my future goals, and I asked God to align my will with His so that I could prosper. I was now controlling my thoughts, and I realized that the tone of my voice had changed also. My heart is now bigger with courage and strength because I've faced many nightmares as dark as the night sky. I am going to school for law so that we can stop being wrongfully imprisoned and murdered not just by each other but also by the law because it seems to have become legal now because cops seem to get away with this. And when a thug, felon or criminal kills each other, I feel the system is glad that this just means one less fool to have to capture.

I have made this a lifetime commitment to never give up on my dreams. I no longer allow others' opinions of me to determine my value, and nothing or no one can take priority over my life again. I am a very amazing woman, and I have so much to give this world, but I had to find myself again after all that has happened to me. I'm an extraordinary woman who will accomplish anything and everything that I set my mind to do. I will settle for nothing less in life. And not only do I recognize this, but I'm also always encouraging and motivating myself to accomplish every opportunity that comes my way. I know what I want out of life, and I'm doing what I want to do in life and loving every moment of it along the way.

I'm a strong young black woman, and it wasn't that I deserve less; I've just accepted less along the way. But now I'm striving to be the best I can be because this lasting impression that my trials and hardships left upon me was just a minor setback for this major comeback that's coming my way. Honest, fair, responsible, and hard-working are what I strive to be. I know my worth, and I walk with confidence because my attitude will determine my direction in life just as it is already showing now.

Since being out, Satan has tried to send everything and everyone close to me up against me (finances, toxic relationships, fake friends and family, snitches as coworkers, sickness, depression, shame and guilt, and my prior criminal record). But in prayer, I will remain faithful toward Jesus Christ. I am wanted because I am irreplaceable. I will be the same yesterday, today, tomorrow, and forevermore. Just ask anyone who knows me. I'm a black girl with a unique name, and I will correct you every time I can see that you are intentionally misleading or causing confusion to someone's life.

Someone believing in me gave me power to mentally and physically change what I didn't like about myself. But just because it looked like I could carry those loads, it doesn't mean that they were not heavy. God allowed me to go through so much pain so that he could prepare me for something far greater, so this was a test to strengthen me. With these tough experiences that I've endured is how I've learned to find light in dark places. It's never too late to change, and when you believe in yourself, you can move mountains.

I'm a stronger woman today because of all my enemies, and the betrayal of fake friends and family that I've endured. It's time for me to be happy and not just be alive but to actually live.

—Takasha L. Stevenson

Independent

Thank you Lord for blessing me with the ability
to make things happen for me and mine.

—Unknown

When the moment had arrived for me to be released from the halfway house, I was able to work however many long hours I wanted to and/or how many jobs I wanted to. However, I chose to work one job in the daytime while I attended school in the nighttime. I had learned from my experience in the halfway house how to sacrifice what I wanted for what I needed. I had watched others around me buy clothing, shoes, jewelry, and wear fancy hairstyles as often as every week, but I wasn't jealous because I knew what my goals were and what needed to be done for me to get there.

I had gone through so much in just a little amount of time after my release because the devil wanted me to quit school, but I couldn't because I knew that school would get me to the success rate that I was reaching for. No, not everyone needs an education to achieve success, but this is what I wanted and felt I needed, especially with a felony on my background. There are lots of people who are very successful and have done it without an education, but trust me, they have some kind of skills, talents or God-given gifts that have helped them along the way. Education, to me, brings about knowledge to help you know the difference between right and wrong and wisdom to know about what is fair and unfair in life. It also helps along the way with stable employment, careers, health insurance, benefits, and resources.

I was thrown into society after serving six months in a halfway house. Little did I have saved because I didn't make much with my job that I worked during my first few months there, which was at Adesa Car Auction in Moody, Alabama, and I only made eight dollars an hour. I had worked this job from November 2017 until February 5, 2018. This was when I got hired with Lear Corporations on February 6, 2018, and I am currently still there as of today.

Two months before my release from the halfway house, I had taken chances and started leaving work early from Adesa Car Auction, looking for an apartment in Hoover. I found one and went through the application process. I got approved for it, but three days later, I received a phone call stating that I was denied because of my felony background. I was hurt, disappointed, and didn't know what to do at this point, and I knew this was one of many no's that I would be receiving in the future because of my felony background.

I knew that I wasn't moving back in my house in Marion, Alabama, because some of the people in that town had put me into prison, and I didn't want to face my oppressors on a daily basis. But also, with the goals I had, there was no way that I could achieve them driving back and forth down that highway every day to work and school.

One of my good friends, whom I am very grateful for today and will forever be grateful for, stepped up after I asked her to get my apartment in her name. She was approved instantly because of her credit and income. I had people to tell me along the way to move back home and into my house because that's where I needed to be. I told them every time they ran in my face with it that I would not unless it was God's will because my attitude toward my witnesses would have me back incarcerated.

I remember when I went and applied for my first car in my own name after my release, and I was scared and didn't know if I would get approved. But I did, and I only had to put down $500 in which I got from my homie, Big Ed, but the note was very high. But it was okay because I had gotten it by my own self, and it was nobody but God in which he gave me favor to get approved with bad credit. And then I was able to give my friend, Shay, her car back.

I had moved my daughter to Hoover with me, and she was in the tenth grade. She didn't want to move away from her family and friends, but she wanted to be with me, so she sacrificed and came with me. Despite my limited income and my staying in a two-bedroom expensive apartment just so that she could attend a safe school in a safe neighborhood while I was away at work during the day and school at night, I will say it again (but God). He kept a roof over our heads, lights, water, and the cable on without me having to beg anyone or go without.

There were times when I needed the help, and God always made a way out of nowhere for someone to give me money just because without me begging and whether it was a boyfriend, friend, family member or stranger, it would be right on time. I would let a bill double to pay for schooling because even though my job offered tuition reimbursement, I had to pay out of pocket at first, and I had to pass with a minimum of a 75/C average to get reimbursed. And besides a roof over my head and transportation, school was my next priority.

There were a few people whom I borrowed from time to time, and I want to acknowledge each of them again: Mike, Tonio, Janika, Pokey, Shay, Cynt and Tracey. I would also like to thank Shervon because every time she would call and invite me out to eat, she would foot the bill because she knew that I hadn't gotten myself quite together yet but wanted to go because seafood was my favorite, and she was the one doing the inviting, knowing I was not financially stable yet. So when I tell you there are good people that still exist today, you better know it.

I also cannot forget my mom because when I tell y'all she has bent over backward for my daughter, whew, I must say she has. I mean there were times when I got jealous and said, "Well darn, you not gonna buy me anything?"

She would just say, "Nope. You are grown. I'm buying your child, so isn't that enough? This should save you."

It took me a while to understand it. I mean, a couple of years or so, but then I started seeing that it was saving me even though she was going to lack some of the stuff anyways because I wasn't going to buy all of them because they were wants and not needs. You see, when it's in God's will, you will know because he will make a way out of no way. I mean, every time I was faced with trials, it was like God parted the Red Sea for me.

There were months when my bills would exceed my income, but I didn't have to go without because it would fall into my hands. And besides, I didn't want to beg because people whom I thought were for me had already let me down many times during my imprisonment and halfway house stay. If God never gives me anything else, the amount that he's given me so far to work with exceeds far greater than I deserve because with His help, I have finally become the person I always wanted to be. I am determined, self-disciplined, and goal-oriented.

On May 08, 2020, all my hard work, dedication, and sacrifices after incarceration had finally paid off. I was able to complete an associate's degree in business administration from Lawson Community College in Birmingham, Alabama, with the financial help of my employer, Lear Corporations, in Tuscaloosa, Alabama, in which they paid for schooling after a year of being employed there, and again on *May 7, 2021,* with a business office management tech/paralegal associate's degree in Tuscaloosa, Alabama.

My cousin, Pokey, also gets kudos because without her keeping my daughter her eleventh and twelfth grade year because after one year, she moved back to our hometown because she was homesick and lonely because of my work and school schedule, I was able to take the maximum amount of credits. It's possible. It could have taken me longer to get my degree because of my child being home alone or I probably would have had to sit out some semesters or not take as many classes. I will use my degree toward my personal and professional goals. My success story goes like this: I have completed a few of my current personal, short-term, professional, graduation, and college-readiness goals.

I am currently enrolled in school again, aiming to achieve a bachelor's degree at Miles College for criminal justice so that I can be accepted into law school in the spring of 2023. I will avoid distractions and stay committed along the way. I do everything with a good heart and expect nothing in return because I have sobbed uncontrollably and have held back tears from the very people whom I thought were like family but let me down along the way. I am now independent and no longer have to depend on anyone for my livelihood. I am free from outsiders controlling me, and no one has authority over me because on November 23, 2020, I was released from my supervised/unsupervised probation due to an early termination because I had done everything right after my incarceration! Oh yeah, and I'm pretty sure the prison overpopulation and COVID had something to do with it! (But God).

> Behind every strong independent woman lies
> a broken little girl who had to learn how to get
> back up and to never depend on anyone!

—Unknown

SOMETIMES you have to LOOSE to WIN again

Fantasia Barrino

After Losing It all

You learn more from your losses, than from your gains.

—Paul Tudor Jones

What is coming is better than what is gone, and in order to receive the new, you have to forget the old. I am not lucky but blessed because everything that I have is because of God's grace and favor on my life. You can't hold on to things illegally or easily gained if you are on God's team. This sudden loss was snatched right from under me because I was betrayed by my daughter's father, whom I thought would at least show up and testify on my behalf to try and save me. But instead, I feel he chose not to because we were no longer together and also because he said he did not want to further incriminate himself. I also was blindsided by old enemies from my past that somehow they were able to resurface and testify falsely against me for the hatred they had against me for other reasons and not for drug trafficking and money laundering in which they exaggerated and lied about. This had hurt me to my core, and it left me stunned.

One day I asked God to open my heart to receive his word and then to give me the strength to obey it. I must admit that I haven't been perfect when it came to helping others. But anybody that knows me, and if they're honest, can say I did my fair share of what I could for those who were in need and with what I had even though I didn't owe them anything. I just had a giving heart because I had been blessed throughout my life because I had dated this man on and off throughout the years, and he took really good care of me.

I had now done my time, and I was ready to move on and get back everything that the enemy had stolen from me because God had already shown it to me in a dream. I was not going to put anything before God again because that's how I lost everything. It wasn't meant to stay because I had gained it with dirty money. How is it that we always put material gain before God when He's the one that gave it to us or allowed us to have it? I had to realize God didn't bless me to ride around in nice cars and to live in fancy housing at the expense of others' downfall or drug addictions.

I used to have a sense of entitlement, but he had now changed all of this to make me become grateful. Two things I have learned for sure that will define a human being is your patience when you have nothing and your attitude when you have everything or shall I say all you need. After my release from the halfway house and when things were not-so-good, I would play gospel songs like "God Provides" by Tamela Mann, "Better Days are Coming" by Le'Andria Johnson, "Never Would Have Made It" by Marvin Sapp, and "I'll Trust You" by Donnie McClurkin because I didn't know how, when or where, but how I had seen God show up and show out for me out of no way possible once before, and whew, child, it blew my mind.

When things were going good for me, I would brag and tell people so that they can know that God did it and not man. I wake up every day grateful and anxious to see what awaits me because things can be temporary and can change in a minute. I had to manage my life on a daily basis and set schedules because my life had become adjusted to pain and losses. I had to focus, motivate, and make commitments to myself to succeed and get back everything that was stolen without relying on others. I thought of starting several businesses, investing, and becoming creative and adventurous because I knew what all I wanted to achieve in life. I have learned an important lesson from pain and losses, and that is pain is unavoidable.

The sense of losing something and never recovering it is a different kind of pain. I lost thirty months in prison and six months in the halfway house that I'll never be able to recover. This has had mental effects on me and will probably follow me the rest of my life because it is permanent and ever present. It can't go away nor can it ever be compensated for. No matter how I distract myself or see the good that has come behind my incarceration, there will always be a deep sense of sadness that will always be with me because the painful reality of the loss will return, which was leaving my children behind parentless because of evil and guilty people who are trying to snitch their way out of trouble and a corrupt justice system that wants convictions and allows them knowing that they're going to just go out and commit another crime!

When I try to not think of it, this only means I have to work harder to suppress it, and it hurts. I've now learned that "the gift of pain is a message about what is important in life." I will now cherish my family, friends, time, and live a meaningful life. Prison was and is a heavy burden that I will carry with me forever, and when someone tells me to get over it, then it becomes even heavier because they are trying to hinder me from healing. I know that those of you who know me honor my courage because I didn't snitch but persevered through it. But I am still left with a burden that's too heavy to carry alone.

Thank you for honoring one of my flaws, and I promise to try and not repeat it. Sometimes I laugh, and other times I'll cry. When I'm accompanied by these thoughts of leaving behind my children over such evil, mean, and grudge-hearted people. I stand strong today with the Armor of God because I can't learn the lesson from loss if I keep running from it. If I fail to learn how to deal with it, then I will continue to suffer silently, fall into depression or continue having panic attacks.

One day I may get better, but there is no delete button that can erase it from my life. I was a victim of Wesley's so-called fake friends who wanted revenge so badly against him that they came after me also. But I will say again, "What man meant for harm, God turned good." I have now walked out of prison whole and better than I was when I went in.

While in prison, I rededicated my life to God. I received a paralegal diploma from Stratford Institute, and I received nine college credits that went toward my associate's degree in business administration that I finished at Lawson College on May 8, 2020. I have been on the same job today for four years since my halfway house time, which is at Lear Corporations. I work at the Serious Injury Law

Group in Birmingham, Alabama, as a part-time paralegal clerk, and I have just graduated a second time on May 7, 2021, from Shelton Community College in Tuscaloosa, Alabama, with a business office management tech/paralegal associate's degree at the time this book was completed.

This is my second book, and I have five more coming in this upcoming year of 2022.

> Wait for the Lord, be strong and let your
> heart stay encouraged, yes wait for the Lord.
> (Psalm 27:14)

Always remember, when it's your time, you'll see God's manifestation in your life.

> In each loss there is a gain, And in every
> gain there is a loss, And with each ending comes
> a new beginning.

—Buddhist proverb

Stress

I will not let someone walk through my mind with dirty feet.

—Mahatma Ghandi

People love giving out free advice and especially when they are not even asked. In the past, this has always led me to always see myself through my family's and friends' eyes and sometimes even my enemies, and at times, this has caused me to be lost. One day I had to seriously ask myself what I allow to define myself. I have learned to stop harming others with my opinions but also not to defend them with my opinions also because this, too, can cause harm.

Labels are for jars and not people, so when you choose healing, you are walking away from those who caused you the stress. Compromising only means that you are settling, dust settles not people so walk away.

Don't stop shining because others are intimidated by your light because when you grow, people will start falling off like the limbs off of trees. Choose people who choose you. I will end any kind of relationship that drains my soul real quick. The more I grow, I learn that others don't understand what's for me is for me. I'm more focused on where I'm going instead of who I'm leaving behind me now. People are who they are. I had to stop giving away my time and energy because I couldn't get it back. People are so quick to call you out for acting funny but catch amnesia when it comes to their actions that contributed to your change.

Before we are healed, God should ask us to give up the things that stress us out in the beginning. We should be made to detox from the very things that made us sick so that we won't go back to them. I had to train my mind, meditate, and read motivational quotes after my release. My whole mindset was now changed. I don't have energy to waste on people or things anymore, so when I feel drained or unhappy, I just remove myself. The way I can cut someone off is far more the scariest thing ever to me because even though I love you, I can live and never talk to you again. And this time, it would be easy because I have already done this before when I was incarcerated for thirty months.

I work very hard to achieve all my goals that I sometimes lack self-care, and I carry a lot of stress around. I don't think anyone could carry a burden around as well as I do except for Jesus. One of the many reasons I act the way I do is because I don't owe anyone an explanation unless I choose to. And if I choose not, then it is what it is. I no longer crave to set the record straight anymore because I will ask for forgiveness and then act as if the problem no longer exists (you). I know that this isn't always good either, but I promised to guard and protect my peace at all times. Accept me or cut me off because I no longer care about losing people who try to disrupt my peace or those who don't want to be in my life anymore.

I've lost people who meant the world to me, and I'm still doing just fine. I'm not easy to come by, replace or forget, so I know that I'll leave a mark on you. Every time my cup has gone empty, it was God who filled it, and I do mean every single time. So I let him fight all my battles now, and I do win them all with Him on my side. It took almost forty years for me to learn, but I now know that the moment you give into others is the moment that you have allowed them to win. It wasn't until I stopped allowing certain people in my life or back into my life more than once to understand this change that had come over me.

The inclination of man's heart is to impress people, but I live now to impress God. We should be turned on and impressed by humility, integrity, generosity, and kindness, and not by our followers, money, degrees, careers, titles, etc. Understand your place with people because shit could kill you if you don't. Always be peaceful, courteous, considerate, respectful, and try to obey the law of the land even when we don't agree and try even harder to obey God's law. Encourage people to stay in good character because God sees and knows all things.

No one sees what you see, even if they can see it too.

The world will not be destroyed by those who do evil acts but by those who watch them without doing anything about it. (Albert Einstein)

This generation is still trying to explain or prove points to their haters, and for whatever reason I'll never understand. Sometimes pain is passed down through the family bloodline until someone decides to let it go. Sometimes so many of us are stressed and under pressure because we are trying to do it all on our own, and this is why we fail every time and we're irritated with those who are always asking but never want to go through what it takes to receive and are always wanting to give advice and haven't been through anything.

Stop, think, kneel, and pray because it's time to get rid of them to save your sanity.

The most expensive liquid in the world is a teardrop and it is made up of 1% water and 99% feelings.

If it doesn't bring you joy, leave it behind. I came up with a plan to balance my life, and I ended up having extra free time.

Pause and remember, every single event in your life, especially the difficult lessons that have made you smarter, stronger, and wiser than you were yesterday.

—Unknown

Reminiscing

There's a reason the windshield is so large, and the rear view mirror is so small. What happened in your past is not nearly as important as what's in your future.

—Joel Osteen

When you step into your future, remember that the enemy will always be there to remind you of your past or he'll get into people and use them to do the job for him! I remember almost every conversation I had with my mom when I would be late arriving somewhere, she would remind me of my past. No matter how I would tell her that was the old me when I lived a life of crime and would be doing wrongful things so I would be lying about my whereabouts because you never knew who would be listening in on phone call (feds), she would still go on and on about it. And it used to get on my nerves. So I would get angry on the inside and not answer her phone calls and wait until I was in a more calm state of mind before answering because I couldn't disrespect my mother.

If I called her and asked her to pay for this or that until I could pay her back, she would do it most of the time but would remind me of how I used to be late on things in my past. Oh boy, how I wished I had someone else to call on to help me instead of her. If I talked with someone in the background while I had her on the phone, she would go on and on about my past and how I hadn't changed and that I was still the same. I don't know what it was with my mom and I when I first got out of prison and after my release from the halfway house also. But I thank God for my stepfather because we almost didn't have the great relationship we have today because Pastor Richard and

Patrice told me when someone is constantly reminding you of your past, they are keeping you stuck in it. So I had to pray really hard to rebuke Satan.

Every time I would go around family members, all they would talk about was something someone had done to them years ago. I don't care which family member it was. It had become repetitive. This was beginning to bother me because at one time, my family was very close, and it seemed like everyone loved each other no matter what was going on. Life is so short, and I had lost my uncle, Arther Stevenson, while I was in prison, so now I intend to spend it with people who make me laugh and make me feel loved. I couldn't take it anymore, so I stayed away from those types of conversations to keep me from reliving the past every day.

I missed out on my daughter's graduation from elementary to middle school in which she became a teenager, and I didn't get out until she was a freshman in high school. And I also missed my son's high school graduation in which he became a young man. I missed my Uncle Arther's funeral. I missed my first and only grandchild's birth into the world and a lot of other painful but precious memories including two handfuls of deaths and funerals of old friends and neighbors from my childhood that I didn't get to pay my respect and say goodbye to.

Those were the things that taught me to hang tight to all of life's memories we make because memories are something that can never be taken away from us. These were things I wanted to reminisce about and not what someone had done five plus years ago because whatever it was, it didn't kill you, and you are still here. Someone whose conversations will always be positive, teaching, encouraging, and motivating is whom I now choose to be around. I work in a factory, and I talk a lot to help make the time pass along, so I won't think of the time clock and going home. I like to have laughing, joking, and serious conversations about life.

I've always been told, "You never know who needs you and good energy is contagious." "Sweet words are good to hear when you've had a rough day." True words aren't always sweet, but no matter what, my smile always helps brighten someone's day because that's who I am.

I always try to stay humble because it's a part of my personality, and so far, it has gotten me showers of blessings from God through many people whom I know and don't know.

I appreciate people's similarities and I respect their differences. People who gossip about other people don't have a life of their own is what I've discovered. When meeting new people about five to ten minutes into the conversation, I can tell their true character. To be honest, I will talk back and forth with people who gossip when it comes to someone I dislike or someone who has wronged me. I won't feed into it too long but just enough to vent and get things off my chest and to get my point across about what wrong the person did to me. I was very careful of what I said to the person I was gossiping with, but at the same time, I was well prepared to answer any question if someone got it back, and the person wanted to confront me about what I had to say.

I used to talk so much and also very loud at times that I would have a sore throat and become hoarse. But for the most part, I try to stay away from gossip now, but I'll also tell you when you're wrong about judging, assuming or guessing. Be careful around certain people who gossip about someone's past because they are reminiscing and basically stuck in the past themselves and love the fact that others are doing bad or worse than them. I try not to talk about my past a lot because the past is just that to me, the past. And besides, mine is too painful, and I want to create new memories. So why waste time on reminiscing about my past and the things that I once had or things that I did wrong when there's a whole big world out there waiting to be discovered unless I'm trying to teach someone and keep them from suffering as I did by giving examples?

When reminiscing, it could sometimes be mentally draining to hear someone stuck in their own past saying what they could have, should have or would have done differently. Oh, if they could turn back the hands of time, some people's lives still would probably be a mess. This will soon consume you, and your thoughts can turn into regrets, and you will start dodging them because you have heard this so much and so many times that you can finish their conversation. When reminiscing, it could also lead you down the wrong roads and have you crossing over many stumbling blocks. When your mind is stuck in the past, this means you have lost your focus. What's behind you is behind you for a reason, so leave it back there unless you are reminiscing about your spouse, children, parents, success or other precious memories.

People who talk about success have great minds. I love meeting new people who are encouraging, motivating, knowledgeable, full of wisdom, care about others, show concern, and don't mind helping you get to the top by sharing their success stories or lending a helping hand. These are the kind of people I love being around because they keep my spirit full and happy. I will talk these kinds of people's ears off. When talking to successful people, I focus on our conversation, and I block out any distractions, and I look into their eyes while conversing. It's like I get a high off of their energy while hearing their success stories. I then go and brag on them like their stories are mine or like they are related to me or are good friends of mine. I want to possess the knowledge these people have, their wisdom, and insight to get ahead in life without experiencing all the hardships.

I love learning new ideas and ways of doing things. I talk a lot because a closed-mouth or close-minded person won't have access to what life has out there. I love to talk to people because you never know what a person is going through and just your conversation alone might save their life. People get worked up over small things when a simple hello or a smile can bring happiness into their life at the moment. God puts people in our life for reasons and for whatever that reason may be, I feel like mine is talking.

Talking is definitely a gift of mine from God. I once was invited to do public speaking at a youth's seminar in Greensboro, Alabama by H.E.R.S., a non-profit organization, for girls ages five to nineteen (founder/CEO is Latavia Hurt). I was nervous, but once I got to telling my story, I loosened up. Little did I know that after graduating high school in May 1998 that I would be back in school over twenty years later taking up business so that I could get a degree and later follow up with criminal justice because I wanted to become a lawyer. I feel my voice was to serve purpose as an attorney, and trust me, they do lots of talking, arguing, and debating. But by the grace of God, I'm ready.

Little did I know that the reason I talked too much and never shut up was a part of my gift. I love to talk, and all my life, I have used my voice to help uplift others in some type of way. I have done public speaking, engaged in short debates at school, and just arguing with friends and family at home. But for whatever the reason, I was just glad to be of help to someone. Who would have ever known that my loud voice would be used as my gift in life to help create my success? Surely not me.

I try to be as wise as serpents but harmless as doves because I don't want to use my wisdom to hurt others but only to correct or teach them. We should judge people by their fruit and accept them as they are and work on being better together. We should join together and stand behind those who are suffering and are lost then point them in the right direction if they would let you because I do understand that everyone doesn't want change, so don't force it. Good people give you happiness. Bad people give you experience. Worst people give you lessons. And the best people give you memories, good talks, and laughs. Oh yeah, that's me.

I love the random memories that make me smile no
matter what is going on in my life at the moment.

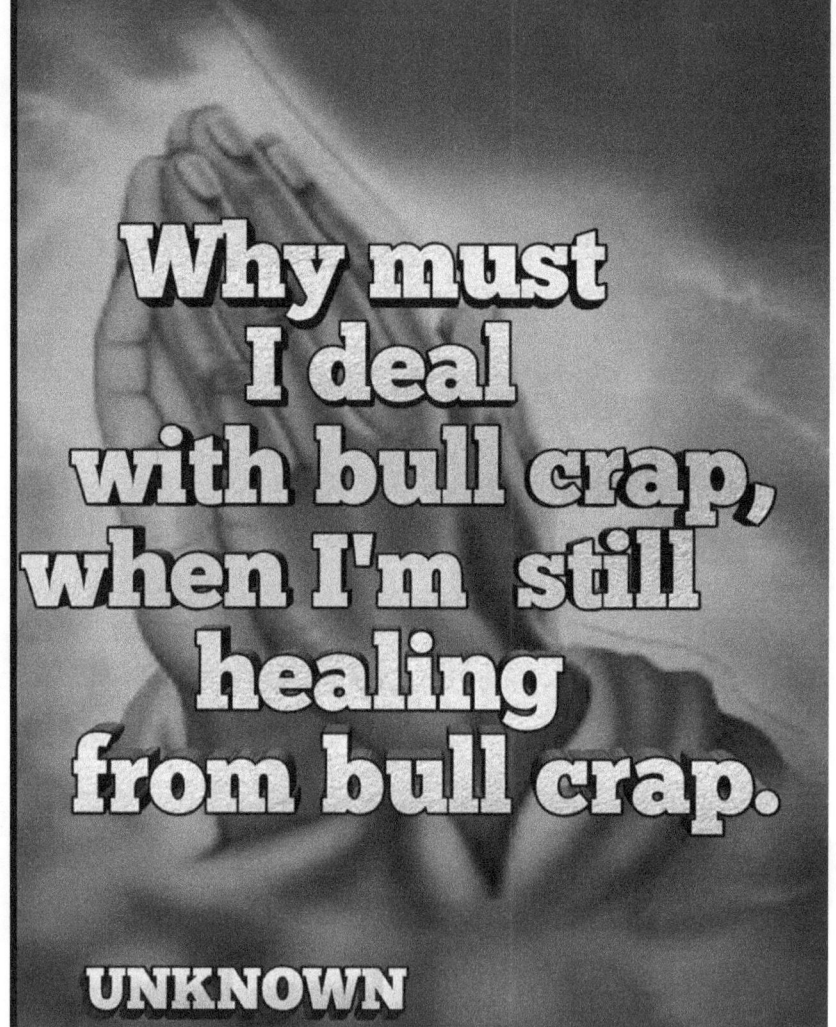

Forgiving

Why must I still deal with bull crap when
I'm still healing from bull crap?

—Takasha Stevenson

I knew that I had not forgiven my enemies when God came to me in a dream and said, *I will turn every bad situation in your life around, bless you and your family, and heal your broken heart.*

I then said, *God, can I watch you get my enemies back for me?*

He said, *What do you mean? I don't have to hurt them for you to see. All I have to do is bless you for them to see.*

I said, *Wow, I feel really bad now. God, I'm sorry.*

He said, *Don't worry, but your blessings will be delayed.*

If I ever get the chance to treat people the way they have treated me, I pray that God will change my heart and that I will walk away. I was like both sugar and salt—one day I would be sweet, and the next day I would be bitter because I was holding hands with misery and becoming a heartless savage.

> Judge not, and you will not be judged; con-
> demn not, and you will not be condemned; for-
> give, and you will be forgiven. (Luke 6:37)

> For from within, out of a person's heart
> come evil thoughts, sexual immorality, theft,
> murder, adultery, greed, wickedness, deceit, lust-

ful desires, envy, comes from within; these things
are what defiles you! (Mark 7:21–23)

I didn't know what had gotten into me, but I'm pretty sure I
knew who (Satan). The hardest part about me forgiving myself was
that I had let others run over me, and I wanted payback.

Don't take it upon yourself to repay a
wrong. Trust the Lord and He will make it right.
(Proverbs 20:22)

But I had to think fast because I was not going to let my past
define me nor was I going to let my enemies win triumph over me
and take away the favor that God has over my life. I was not about
to let anything or anyone hold me back from all that I had promised
God I would achieve anymore. I was now a better version of myself,
and I had to tell myself over and over again sometimes it just looks
like others are doing fine when in reality they are not because you
never know what goes on behind closed doors in other's lives.

I spent several months trying to figure out what was wrong with
me until I realized that all I needed to do was condition my mind
because it was unforgiveness there that had me in this state of being.
Revisiting my past was hurtful to my mind and heart because they
are connected. All my life I have heard the words forgive and forget,
but I can assure you all my life I have never forgotten when someone
has done me wrong, not one person. I may have not gotten revenge
against them all, but trust me when I say I can remember it all, and I
mean down to every little detail.

Every time I look back, I digest every hardship I've endured all
over again. Every facet of my past is flawed in my eyes. You must let
go is something that I find myself repeating over and over again. But
to act as if my past didn't exist would be like discrediting God for
bringing me through it all. My prison moments were not a reflection
of who I am because my identity now does not agree with my past
situation. The old Kasha did what the culture wanted me to. It made
me chase after things that made my name (Kashmny) great. While

searching for my identity, I had to stop condemning myself. So many times I've thought to myself, I wished I had not given so much of my time to people and helped them as I did before prison, but I think this was why I also got a lot of help from God when I got out because of all I've done in my past.

I may have wasted time and money, but you could never give someone too much love. Judging, identity, and forgiveness go together. So be careful when you speak ill of someone else because words can only be forgiven and not erased. Everyone around me was questioning me, and it seemed like some were even being nosy, while others were trying to break me down by revisiting my past. Others still bringing up my past made it hard for me to forgive myself most of all. I always found myself repeating, "Let them try it now or I bet they won't do that bull crap now."

But I will never go back to who I used to be even though the old me still lives in me. I had to create a safe place in my life and remove myself from around people, and it was then that I could see. I have faced a dark past, and I'm very good at reading people, so I try to protect everyone I love because I have overcome many obstacles. So this makes me stronger than before. I have faced many struggles in life, so when you abuse my trust, the old me will make you regret losing me.

The enemy is still after my character, mind, and understanding till this very day, so I have to fight with everything in me at all times because once again, he wants to have his way with me again. I know the only way to overcome it is to retrace my old steps so that I could make better choices this time around. My passion has now become mistaken for aggressiveness to some people, but I am unapologetic about it all because I am still struggling to forgive myself at times. If others cannot recognize that I have changed, it's okay because I am not going to waste time explaining myself or trying to prove anything to anyone.

Forgiveness is like getting rid of poison in your soul to become healthy again. I no longer dislike people but will probably always dislike the things that we as people do and say, especially when we know better. I have forgiven everyone who has wronged me, even my cousin whom I said could go to HELL and anyone defending him could also go because what he had done taught me an important lesson. And that's never depend on man/woman again and always have a backup plan because two is always better than one, and I've also forgiven my enemies again and again and again because without them, you wouldn't be reading this book.

I have planned now to live an unapologetic life, and if someone can't understand this, then they don't need to be in my presence. Now I live with strength, and I laugh without fear of the unknown, and I love like I've never been hurt because I've experienced great pain and losses in my past. I now have dignity, but in the end, I found that all my strength came from above. I've learned that when you are obedient and faithful to God, nothing can stop what He has for you. I stay ready in and out of season.

> To forgive is to set a prisoner free and
> discover that the prisoner was you.
>
> —Lewis B. Smedes

Freedom

Our greatest freedom is the freedom to choose our attitude.

—Viktor Frankl

How can you appreciate freedom if you've never been bound before? My freedom had been stripped away from me because my rights were violated, and I did not feel I had a fair trial because all my enemies became my witnesses and testified falsely against me in which they told lies and exaggerated the truths in some things. My rights to equality before the law were violated because my privacy was invaded and twisted onto a falsification document (spreadsheet). So why didn't they use the actual bank statements that were subpoena because this would have helped me remember better than a document (spreadsheet) with numbers and dates, which could have been used for anything. The original bank statement showed you exact transactions to whom, what, and where.

I tossed and turned in my bed many nights as I thought to myself about the hand I was dealt in life, the poor choices I had made, the lack of family support I had as a young lady while growing up, and it just made more and more sense for me to bald up and cry at night. I could only think of the two innocent children I had left behind, Rj and Wes. I was shackled in my mind from guilt, shame, regret, and the embarrassing moment of being handcuffed in front of them in the courtroom. When I arrived at the halfway house, the little rights I had gained back were taken away again because of the degrading treatment from Ms. Jaye, the director. What I thought was freedom actually wasn't.

After my release from the halfway house, I couldn't go where I wanted to without having to ask permission, so was I really free is what I thought on many days. I was able to think and speak as I wanted, but I couldn't act as I wanted because of certain restraints I had attached to my name, and I belonged to a certain class now (felons). Getting out of prison doesn't make you free because with your background, it's hard to find a job, car, housing, etc., and you still have to check in with a probation officer each month. My freedom was a demonic probation, meaning freedom with strings attached.

Freedom, to me, is being able to control my own actions without authority looking over my shoulder. So my freedom after my release wasn't so beneficial because I couldn't leave the state or country without permission, and I couldn't vote for the upcoming 2020 Presidential election in which I would have voted for Joe Biden and Kamala Harris, by the way.

My freedom went like this most of my first year of release from the halfway house. I was awakened each morning by my alarm for work, and I would see the sunrise. And I took a few minutes to stare at the view from my window. I would sit in my living room and reflect on how I felt because I was now able to sit in that space alone without having to hear others yapping their big mouths and not being considerate of the other inmates in the TV room. I recited a positive quote each morning for affirmation that related to me, and I would listen to a song that related to my situation. I wore clothing of my choice that made me feel confident in my own skin as to who I was after prison. I took a bubble bath because I was now able to sit down in a tub, which I couldn't do in prison. They only had showers. I touched on my body parts each day and night because I was able to see them as a whole because the prison only had half mirrors, and I had to jump up or stand on something to see my whole body.

I would drive longer routes to my destination to enjoy the scenery. I would cry out loud each time my feelings and emotions took over me, and I would put my hand on my heart to feel each heartbeat to make sure it was real, and I was still alive. As of today, I don't do all the things I did right after my release anymore, but some new things I do today are: I set a positive intention for the day. I visualize how it'll go my way. I focus hard on what my energy is worth, and I protect it by trusting my instincts. What I'm in training and learning to do now is make an effort to slow down when I'm in a rush because accidents are prone to happen in these instances. I've started writing down five of my most important values each week. I've started writing down three things that worry me but is out of my control and give them over to God.

I'm trying not to do but an hour on social media each day, exercise for thirty minutes a day to stretch and relax, write down three things and people who inspire me to be great. I dance and sing like no one is watching while I'm getting ready for work each day because I missed twerking as they call it now. I drink more water. This may be simple to some of you, but this is what freedom means to me—being me in my own skin. When God gets you out of the dark, people, let's not forget him. Difficulty only means that you haven't figured it out yet, but don't go backward.

I was now free and able to live a meaningful life, which was pleasing to me and God, so I definitely did not want to disappoint him. I was able to pick up pieces that I had buried and was now able to express myself through my many books I will write and in any way I choose about what and whom I choose if you played a part in my life, whether good or bad. So live like everyone is watching you, especially me. I love to write because I don't have to worry about any interruptions (my thoughts).

It's not about the time you have. It's about what
you'll do with the time you have left?

—Timothy Alexander

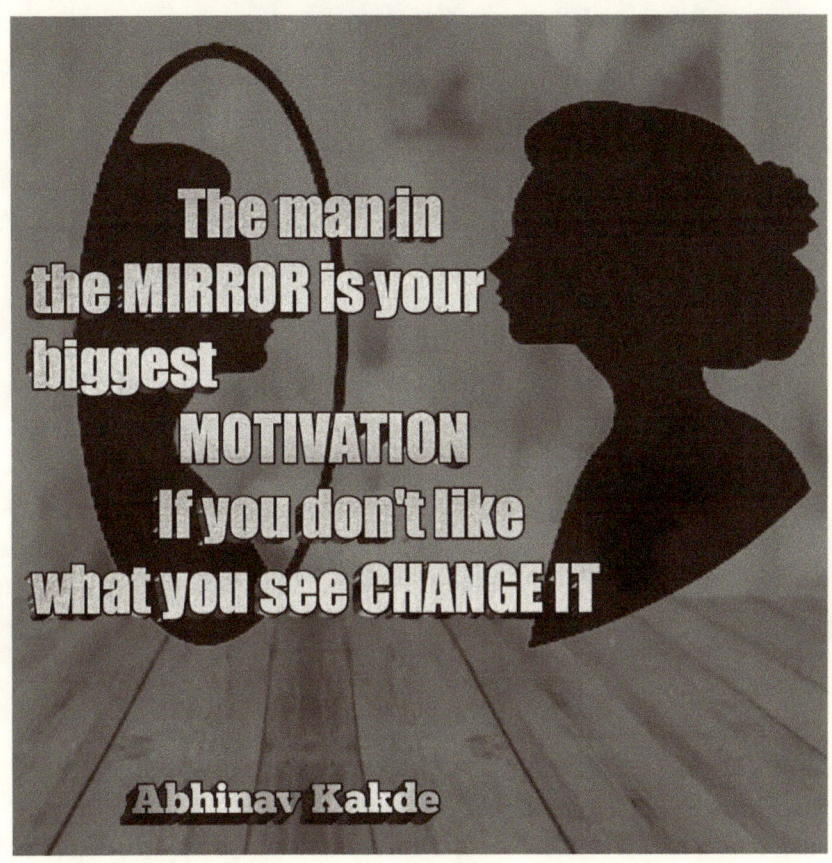

Man in the Mirror

If you're always looking for the next best thing
then you'll never see what's in front of you.

To the outside world who didn't know, but I once was a heart broken, unhappy, suffering, and miserable young lady trying to hold together a fool's paradise in the public's eye before prison. I had gone down the wrong paths in life but had now been rehabilitated because of my incarceration. Throughout life, I had experienced an unbalanced give and take lifestyle, so my instinct was usually I'll figure it out on my own because I didn't want to ask anyone. Life has now taught me that you cannot control someone else's loyalty to you.

> Everything in life is upon your ability and capacity to understand appropriately and adequately through certain people, times and seasons.

I feel that age has nothing to do with your purpose in life, but timing is everything, so find your season and adjust to it as I did. I was buried under cultural conditioning of other's opinions and inaccurate information. Who I was and what I did were two separate things, so why was I still being labeled by my past behavior and when were things going to change? When I would come out of my room at the halfway house, I would be told to go back in and change my pants because they were too tight and there were guys at this facility also. But then when you look at some of the staff that worked there, their clothes were tighter fitting than mine. I know what you're thinking, great example right!

I remember being out in the sitting area one day, and I was told to go back inside my dorm because there were too many men in the lobby, and one of them had come and sat down at my table. So I went up to the officer and said, "No, I will not because I was sitting at the table first, and the lobby was empty when I came out, so why not make him get up and leave?"

He raised his voice at me, and I reminded him that I was thirty-seven years old and also an adult with two children of my own, and a grandbaby and that I wasn't in prison anymore, so stop treating me like I was. I almost lost my cool with him that day, and I could have ended up in the county jail because my mouth gets really disrespectful when I feel I'm being misjudged and especially targeted, so that's why I don't like to argue. Was it because I was a felon and he thought that because my clothes were too tight I would sleep with strangers? Or was it because he thought I had no self-respect and that I would sleep with strangers?

I told him, "Well, I knew what it was. You thought that I would do anything because I had been locked up for years in prison and that us felons would come out and would do anything because we were now back into the free world!" Well, I don't know what type of women he had been used to dealing with in the past at this facility, but still you should not judge all felons by one or previous felons. Of course, he denied it, but what reason did he have to send me back into my room? Because the lobby was full of men? Hell, in the free world, I would be around more men than the ones in the halfway house at a time. It wasn't my fault that I was in a coed halfway house facility and that there were only two other women there with me who loved to stay shut up in their rooms. Well, not me because I had had enough of being confined.

Because of certain types of disrespect toward me, I have to constantly remind myself to be a voice and not an echo. I have never been afraid to raise my voice for honesty, truth, compassion, injustice, lying, greed, picking, bullying, etc. At this point, I didn't want to do right anymore. And because of this one of many incident, I had now started struggling to do right because it had caused me to not think clearly anymore. Why must I continue to do right when everyone wants to pick at me? I may as well become who they think I am because it was clear evidence that they must have looked down on me because I had just been released from prison after serving two and a half years.

People should watch how they talk to one another and also how they treat them because you will have to answer to God if you cause someone to fall or stagnate with your opinions or judgement.

> Therefore let us not pass judgement on one
> another any longer, but rather to decide never to
> put a stumbling block or hindrance in the way of
> a brother. (Romans 14:13)

I had wondered if these people had seen me as a failure. I had to catch myself several times and not get caught up in the flesh by having the right intentions but miss a step because of what others had to say about me. I had to continue making choices about who I was by recognizing who I was not, and it wasn't fair for me to always have to defend myself.

> Confusion comes from how someone sees
> you or wants you to be and others agreeing to it
> helps influence it.

As people, we need to start focusing on someone's abilities and not their inabilities. People don't change who they are, but our perception of them surely can. I had to get alone with God again and find myself because I was tired of being misjudged by my appearance and/or my past. Every night I spent in that halfway house, which was five months, I was being misjudged by all of the employees that worked there except for maybe five of them with three being men all because of my figure (shape) in which our creator had designed me.

While people have so many negative things to say about one another, I wonder have we ever thought to ourselves that we didn't design ourselves and that God did? Because if I had, I would have given myself more titties! I had already learned how to love myself, and it was a tough process to go through, so I didn't need any reminders from anyone. Finding myself was a process, and my change didn't come overnight because I certainly didn't lose myself overnight. When I began loving myself more, my relationships with people started to change also, and there were certain people I couldn't stand to be around anymore because I had outgrown them.

Who I was and who I am becoming are two different people as well because God is not finished with me yet. Seasons come to change you by transforming your thinking and behavior. I evaluate myself daily to make sure that my mouth matches my life's pursuit because God is more concerned about my character than my accomplishments. I once had a false identity attached to my name because of how someone saw me. Life is about how we are taught, so when you are taught wrong and no one challenges you or tell you that you are incorrect, how will you know that you're incorrect?

People have oftentimes underestimated me, and they don't even know what all I have been through. I have a fighting spirit, and I have given up so much to keep my children and myself safe. Going to prison was the second time I had allowed my kids to live with a relative or my best friend. The first time I had left them behind was to get away from my daughter's father because he was abusive, and he stalked me even after our relationship was over. Yes, I was stalked by the man I had served time in prison for. I had to leave my two kids behind to prepare a safer place in another city for us to live and so that I wouldn't kill him or get killed by him because the police wouldn't do anything about it because they didn't have the proof (evidence) of what he was doing to me.

After doing this, I heard so much talk about how I didn't have time for my children anymore, and the saddest part was, it came from the people who were most close to me. Nobody ever sat down with me one time to see what I was going through as a single woman/ mother by continuing to run away from this man and after leaving a brand new home I had built in 2009, three years earlier before I had moved away nor did they try to help me protect myself and my children from this man after finding out what he was like but instead had so much to say about the material things (house) I had left behind along with my kids and about the material things I were buying.

I have always hid my hurt from the world because my anger is so powerful, and it's unstoppable once it's been unleashed. I am not the typical chick to try and control nor do I want to have control over others. I am a light that shines so bright, and I always win others over because I know how to both empathize and sympathize with them. Despite all that I've been through, I am beautiful inside and out because I have a generous, kind, giving heart and soul. I am beautiful to look at but most dangerous if you rub me in the wrong way. I treat all with respect even when it's not earned or deserving because I have remarkable kindness toward the human race. I'm very considerate, and I'm not rude unless provoked, and then I'll act as if I'm untamed. I'll be like a flame of fire that can't be put out no matter how hard you blow it.

I had now stepped into a season of answered prayers by being released from the halfway house, and I was trying to become who I wanted to attract. Self-respect is like rent, and it's owed out and due every day from everyone. I live with a protective instinct now because I have to guard my heart against pretenders (those who pretend to care to get the inside scoop). I vowed to hang out with others that can help me learn the relevancy of living a loving and healthier lifestyle so that I can always recognize my worth! I live, laugh, and I still cry when I'm alone. I have a smile that would brighten your saddest day.

I'm very sensitive but don't think I'm a pushover because I'm stubborn as well because I'm almost always right. I'm very loyal to anyone who is family or to whom I consider a close friend. I'm not stuck-up. I'm straight forward, and I don't have patience for nonsense or games. When I used to look in the mirror, I saw pain, mistakes, and heartache. But now when I look in the mirror, I see strength, beauty, and learned lessons. I'm so proud of myself. I'm Kashmny, a free natural born leader. That's me!

You'll never see all the awesome things in front of you if you keep looking at all the bad things behind you. Sometimes you just have to turn around, give a little smile, throw the match, and let it burn. Live, learn, and don't look back unless it's to wave goodbye!

Good friends
are hard to find,
harder to leave
and impossible
to forget.
G. Randolf

Real Friends

Good friends are like stars, you don't always
see them but know that they are there!

—Christy Evans

It's not the people who let us down, it's our expectations of them. Fake friends don't love you. They only love what you can do for them. I had to cut a few people off because everyone was not meant to grow with me because I had outgrown them. You cannot make people act right, but when you cut them loose, they will wish they did even though it will be too late. But trust me, they will know how to treat the next person.

I'm not fighting for a role in anyone's life
when the show is all about me.

People can lie on you and assassinate your character, but your good deeds will always be there to speak for themselves. These kinds of persons should be deleted from your personal space and unfollowed on social media. Don't answer calls or texts. Better yet, they should not even have your phone number. Walk away from them and do not look back. Remember what happened to Lot's wife in the Bible. She turned into a pillar of salt for looking back (Genesis 19:26).

This is what happens to us as humans. We become salty because we chose to deal with people again after we have forgiven them for crossing us. You cannot force anyone to pay you back with the same loyalty you gave away. You cannot force others to give you the same love and respect you gave to them. They are not obligated to treat or value you in the same way you gave to them. After my release, I could see clearly who was there for me, who was against me, and who was there for a publicity show to say they gave me a helping hand after I got released. So I turned many of them down.

It didn't take me long to see through these kinds of people because their words said something different than what their actions showed me. I also learned another important lesson: If you want to know who your real friends are, just get yourself into some trouble and depend on them to get you out and see who will stay around and who will leave.

"A choir director has to turn his back on his audience." But in a time of need, you should be able to depend on a friend. While I had been transformed into the likeness of God, I received insight, wisdom, and revelation about myself and others in which I now look at things in a new way. Before prison, I helped those closest to me. But while in prison, I found out some of them were lost in the world, and that's why I had to help them, and they couldn't help me back because that's why they had needed my help.

My actions have always been questionable to others, but I don't know why because I have always done whatever I could to help someone else in need. I've now learned what kind of relationships, companionship, friendship or intimacy was essential in my life. I've made a significant change in my life, but I always try to remember where I used to be before God cleaned me up so I won't prejudge too hard. I prayed to God to reveal my enemies to me so that I won't fear them but be cautious around them.

The Bible speaks of "the kisses of an enemy is deceitful." So I had to be very cautious because I had people right under me trying to ruin my name. Find those people who are for you because T.D. Jakes says it best:

> Confidants are those who love you uncon-
> ditionally. Constituents are those who are not
> into you but into what you are for, and as long
> as you are into what they are into, they will be

around. But when somebody new comes around, they will leave you for them. And last, comrades are not for you and not what you are for but are against what you are against and will team up with you to fight a common enemy, but after the battle they will leave you. So be careful and get you a confidant.

The problems that came with me being who I am today I can certainly say were challenging. I had some very loving and kind-hearted people who were really in my corner, and I must say, their actions have left an impressionable mark on my heart forever. My mom showed up and did her thing for my daughter, which helped me tremendously. My cousin/sister, Pokey, took my daughter under her wing, which allowed me to work long overtime hours and attend school after work. My Aunt Sarah opened her home and let me stay with her and do home confinement on my weekend passes from the halfway house and also my last thirty days before my release with an ankle monitor on. My best friends, Shay and Cynt, went out the way for me continuously after my release from the halfway house for my survival.

But I must say, through it all I learned a valuable lesson. God has brought me too far to stop trusting Him and give up now. He has given me a deep understanding of two is better than one and can catch each other when one falls. But this doesn't work with every-body because nowadays people are always looking out for handouts like they are owed! I'm finally in a place in my life where if I have to watch my back from someone around me and in my inner circle, then this gives me reasons to end the relationship/friendship because, "Cain killed Abel and that was his blood brother." (Genesis 4:8)

I would rather walk with a friend in the dark, than alone in the light because believe it or not but this is why so many are alone, miserable and hating from frustration of trying to do it all on their own why it looks like others are living their best life!

Conclusion

Everyone has a story to tell because it holds history so that you won't ever forget where you come from, where you are now, and to remind you to never go back to what you've been delivered from. I once was broken into many pieces, and now I'm sharing my story so that the world can know what it was like to face the real and true pain that had threatened to run the very fabric of who I once thought I was.

When I arrived at the halfway house, I didn't have anything but a house in which was being rented out in Marion, Alabama, to one of my cousins, old clothes I had left behind and were now too small. I didn't have a car to get around, and I didn't have anything besides the thirty-five-dollar debit card in which the prison had released me with. I had walked out of prison with a temporary debit card. My incarceration was a defining moment that shifted me from the free world to a (6x9) prison cell by guilt of association (conspiracy). It greatly impacted my thinking as to making wise choices and decisions now as well as flourishing my maturity. Along with my maturity and renewing of the mindset came the way I represented and carried myself. It was displeasing and distasteful to some, but others' opinion of me didn't matter anymore because I was responsible for me.

I've now gotten over blaming everyone around me for not wanting to give me help to keep certain things that were necessities and losing everything I own, except for my house. I now choose to put myself first everyday but not by being selfish but by understanding that the letter I comes before the letter U in the alphabets. So if I am not straight, how can I get you straight? We both will go down. I've learned to choose the pain of discipline over the pain of regret. My life was constantly changing because I was taking advantage of the opportunities life had to offer a felon. I've now repositioned myself to grow so that I can receive all that God has for me.

My mistakes were my lessons as well as my blessings but in disguise. I am searching for inner peace and telling my stories so that others can overcome their obstacles and heal with me. God has entrusted me with the gift of speaking, so I want to be the very best at it. Experience is the best teacher because how can you tell someone how to get through something if you've never been through it yourself? But wisdom can come from you reading this book and learning from my mistakes. I've planned to use this experience to improve the lives of others around me.

I became who I am today by making a conscious decision not to allow my circumstances that had put me in prison to follow me the rest of my life. Now that I am changed and have overcome adversities, God is using me in all areas of my life where I am clean to help someone else. Notice I did say clean. My prison experience encouraged me to have compassion and care for those who are lost in the world and are less fortunate. It helped me to seek answers to the questions who, what, when, where, and why about life afflictions. Who I was before and after my incarceration is nothing compared to who I am today.

I am solid physically, mentally, spiritually, and financially because I don't treat others how they treated me, and I pray for detachment from all things that pull me away from God. No matter how many doors man had shut on me, God opened them all plus many more. He allowed me to walk back into the same job that I had before my imprisonment except with a different company. He allowed me to receive two associate's degrees. He allowed me to publish two books as of now, with five more on the way. He has blessed me to be financially stable and not have to depend on others. He has blessed me with great health, and my grandmother, mother, and children are all living and healthy. I have a great support system to this very day from friends and some family but also with a very special guy whom I just love.

Be careful how you treat people, especially the ones you don't think you need. Being humble will take you places that money just cannot!

Never forget three types of people because they were necessary.

Never forget those who put you in your difficult times (enemy/frenemy), those who left you in your difficult times (fake friends and family), and those who helped you in your difficult times (real friends, family, and strangers).

Until

Until you've been arrested,
And spent endless days in jail,
And walked a hundred miles,
Without ever leaving your cell

Until you've lost your family,
And you're utterly alone
You try to seek comfort,
Realizing it was left at home

Until you've faced a judge,
And entered your guilty plea
And you've heard the words of judgement,
That you won't be going free

Until your days turn into months,
And months turn into years
You lie awake at night,
Shedding endless tears

Until you've lost all hope,
And every dream you've ever had
You fight to keep your sanity,
And fear that you'll go mad

CONVICTION TO CORRECTION

Until you've gone through all these things
And lost all human will,
How can you look at me and say
You know just how I feel?

—Anonymous

A New Message to My Hometown

Everyone has a role to play in this world, whether it is good or bad. We need to put our issues aside and address the issues and not people. People no longer stick together anymore and stand up for what's right but rather turn a blind eye because it doesn't affect them. It's time for a change, and change starts with one's own self, but you also have to want change and then make a change.

Working toward change doesn't guarantee your life will change for the better, but you have to invite it and embrace it, find your voice, and take a stand. Society has taught us to ignore the ills we see and leave it to someone else to make the change until it affects them or their family. And then they want to cry for help. We also don't take time to address the issues properly because we feel no one will listen. No one can take care of a community better than those who resides there or those who have come from there. Community is best when everyone is engaged, respects and listens to where the other person comes from. Everyone should have a voice to speak up and speak out.

There was a time when parents appreciated the neighborhood for correcting their children. But today you can hardly say anything to someone else's kids for looking down the barrel of a shotgun, but I must admit there are some people out there who will speak disrespectfully to our children. But this should be when we step to the adult. It takes a village to raise a child because they are victims already because of circumstances from their neighborhood, environment or parents. I believe generational curses help our children go down the wrong paths due to no fault of their own.

Where are all the Black mothers gone? Motherhood is a privilege and puts you in a position of leadership. Where are all the Black fathers today? Fatherhood is a privilege and puts you in a position of power. Children are blessings from the Lord that carry on for many generations and become adults. Children are our future, and we should help them along the way because raising them isn't just a financial responsibility, it's about spending quality time together, preparing meals, teaching them right from wrong, and most importantly, how to respect themselves and others! This should be crucial to everyone because they are our future!

The Skin I'm In

We as black people are already discriminated against because of the color of our skin or how we appear to be. So let's stop fighting amongst each other and worry about our common enemy. In today's society, I truly feel that information about black people is over and understated. This happens when other races feel strongly about their beliefs or have been taught this way.

In today's society, a lot of information on blacks is assumed, misstated, exaggerated, and dramatized. This world could possibly change if people started collecting and gathering factual information (evidence) and letting go of interpretations and opinions (assumptions). Developing this attitude and behavior is hard at first, but it's the start of a change. If we set aside our beliefs, feelings, values, thoughts, and focus on the real views and experiences, which is blacks killing each other, and then we can come together to fight our common enemy (racism).

Let us not then forget our past but let go because it is behind us now. We need to start living in the present and spend time correcting these misperceptions so that we can stop getting viewed as thugs, gangsters, and criminals, and then we can live longer lives. Maybe if we set aside our feelings and attend to society's needs, we can understand but not fully agree with those who see the world differently from us. So let's start by opening your eyes to what you love to hate!

About the Author

Takasha has served thirty months in Greenville Federal Prison Camp in Greenville, Illinois, and six months at the Birmingham Halfway House Correctional Facility. She is originally from Marion, Alabama. After her release, she reunited with her family, and she moved her daughter to Hoover, Alabama, when she was a sophomore in high school but has now finished up her senior year and is a high school graduate class of 2021.

Since her release from prison, she has received two associate's degrees—one in business administration and the other in business office management tech/paralegal—with the help of her employer's, Lear Corporations, tuition reimbursement program, and she is proud to say she's still there today almost four years later after her release. She also works part-time at a law firm, Serious Injury Law Group, in Birmingham, Alabama, as a paralegal clerk. She is continuing her education in psychology and criminal justice and wants to advocate for the proper rehabilitation programs to be put into place to help reduce crime and reduce the recidivism rate from rising.

Since her release, she has endured attacks from enemies as well as fake friends and family whom she thought would repay her with the same loyalty she had or would have shown toward them if the tables were turned. Despite these stumbling blocks that were thrown her way, she tackled them all. One problem and one day at a time. She did not let this break her in the end, and she has shown forgiveness and love through it all!

She is now patient and thinks thorough and rational before making decisions because she realizes that your life can change in a split second! She now lives by the words, "Help me help you and just because you don't see anything happening, doesn't mean GOD is not working on your behalf. If we want change, then we have to change it by being that change!"

Printed in the USA
CPSIA information can be obtained
at www.ICGtesting.com
LVHW052032230524
781050LV00017B/36